ROYAL FRAUD

ROYAL FRAUD

The Story of Albania's First and Last King

Robert C. Austin

Central European University Press
Budapest—Vienna—New York

©2024 Robert C. Austin

Published in 2024 by
CENTRAL EUROPEAN UNIVERSITY PRESS

Nádor utca 9, H-1051 Budapest, Hungary
Tel: +36-1-327-3138 or 327-3000
E-mail: *ceupress@press.ceu.edu*
Website: *www.ceupress.com*

Cover illustration: Undated painting of Zog the First, King of the Albanians by Spiro Xega. Photo courtesy of the Albanian State Central Archives, Tirana.

Cover and book design by Sebastian Stachowski

ISBN 978-963-386-710-5 (paperback)
ISBN 978-963-386-711-2 (ebook)

LIBRARY OF CONGRESS CATALOGING-IN-PUBLICATION DATA

Names: Austin, Robert C., author.
Title: Royal fraud : the story of Albania's first and last king / Robert C. Austin.
Description: New York : Central European University Press, 2024. | Includes index.
Identifiers: LCCN 2023053236 (print) | LCCN 2023053237 (ebook) | ISBN
  9789633867105 (paperback) | ISBN 9789633867112 (adobe pdf)
Subjects: LCSH: Zog I, King of the Albanians, 1895-1961. | Albania--Kings and rulers-
  -Biography. | Albania--History--1912-1944. | BISAC: HISTORY / Europe / Eastern
Classification: LCC DR974 .A87 2024 (print) | LCC DR974 (ebook) | DDC
  949.65/02092 [B]--dc23/eng/20231120
LC record available at https://lccn.loc.gov/2023053236
LC ebook record available at https://lccn.loc.gov/2023053237

Table of Contents

Acknowledgements

I am grateful to so many people for their guidance and encouragement. At the University of Toronto, my friends at the Centre for European, Russian, and Eurasian Studies at the Munk School of Global Affairs and Public Policy, Randall Hansen, Larysa Iarovenko, Olga Kesarchuk, Katia Malyuzhinets and Edward Schatz, give a whole new meaning to collegiality, loyalty, and friendship. Ksenya Kiebuzinski was the best librarian as always. Gratitude also goes to several research assistants in Toronto: Isabelle Avakumovic-Pointon, Oya Darici, Ana Djordjijevic, Tami Piovesan, Madeliene Schmuckler, Amelie Tolvin, and Tatiana Velickovic.

At the University of Regensburg, where I was a visiting fellow in 2022 at the Leibniz-Institut für Ost- und Südosteuropaforschung, thanks to Ulf Brunnbauer, Heike Karge, and Paul Vickers for providing a place to talk about Zog, Albania, and the Balkans among the world's best experts. In Vienna, where much of the book was finalized, thanks to my friends at the Institut für die Wissenschaften vom Menschen (IWM) where I spent six wonderful months in 2023 as a visiting fellow. The whole team there created a unique intellectual oasis. Special thanks to Desislava Gavrilova, Misha Glenny, Ivan Krastev, and Ivan and Spomenka Vejvoda.

Enormous assistance also came from two young historians: Artan Hoxha in Tirana and Alessandro Sette in Bari. Both gave up time to help me find things but also got me to see things differently. What started out as emails grew into wonderful new friendships and collaboration.

ACKNOWLEDGEMENTS

At the Central European University Press, Senior Editor Linda Kunos saw the value of the book straight away. From our first meeting in Budapest in May 2023, her professionalism and devotion were clear.

Finally, thanks to my family. Our children, Andrew and Kate, give me so much to be proud of and my wife, Maureen, makes everything possible.

The story that follows is dedicated to them.

Chapter One

Endings and Beginnings

Likely few people could recall that Albania once had its own homegrown king who apparently said little but survived the most dangerous period in European history. Even before Albania was a kingdom it was often a mere curiosity. In 1912, when it declared independence from the Ottoman Empire, newspapers likened Albania to "Darkest Africa" with its gun-toting mountaineers, blood feuds, veiled women, and sheep. When it became a kingdom in 1928, with a self-declared King Zog I, the snickering continued. After the king fled in 1939 and later under communist rule, *Time* magazine would call it the "most wretched country in Europe." The CIA would note that Albanians are a "turbulent people, always willing to fight for hire or for loot." Albanians are easily the most maligned people in Europe.

By the time the communists finally surrendered power in 1991 and Albania began a fraught and brutal transition to its own brand of market capitalism that looked more like a circus, the one-time king was long dead. However, in November 2012, a coffin with the mortal remains of King Zog I went home to be reburied in Tirana after 51 years in a French cemetery. November 2012 was an auspicious date for Albania—they were celebrating the centenary of independence, and their one and only true king had been there from the start. Whether they liked him or not, Albanians could not deny that in the twentieth century there were only two people who mattered, and Zog was one of them. The other, the formally revered and feared but by then much-despised communist dictator Enver Hoxha, who ruled between 1944 and 1985, had already been disgraced and in 1992 summarily removed from his hallowed grave overlooking Tirana to a place among the commoners. Odd that in the span of twenty years, the two leading Albanians had been dug up and, in a way, changed places. It was clear that Albanians still loved "strongman" rule; they just had to change the "strongman" occasionally.

Between the First and Second World Wars, Zog, a particularly enigmatic figure, known early on for his bravery in the Balkan Wars and the First World War but later for his laziness and love of pomp, emerged to dominate the entire period in a country that had witnessed multiple changes in government but hardly any change. He was an able interior minister, then prime minister, then president, and, in 1928, self-proclaimed King of the Albanians. His claim to the throne was spurious and based on lies that in some ways foreshadowed the cults of personality that would be associated with later communist rulers. The decision to become king was based on a few things: the Balkans were mostly run by kings, plus Zog wanted to impress his mother, and he was equally eager to provide his six sisters with easy upward social mobility.

Once king, his accomplishments were decidedly meager, although his admirers credited him with some role in making the Albanian nation and state. He was largely shunned by other royal families, even the less than regal ones in places like Bulgaria or Romania. He spent most of his time keeping up appearances as a monarch, despite the obvious fraud he had imposed on an illiterate and uninterested population. His one great success was in having almost all of his opponents murdered, mostly in broad daylight in foreign countries.

He got rich by taking bribes from everyone, especially Benito Mussolini. He pocketed the sale of Albania's assets. After nearly being assassinated in Vienna in 1931, he never left Albania again but largely hid out in his palace until Mussolini's army forced him into exile. He certainly left Albania almost as he found it—feudal, mostly illiterate, and poor.

Despite the stunning lack of achievements, Zog's story tells a wider story of Europe from the periphery in a time of enormous precarity. Albania's survival was never assured, and neither was Zog's. Neighbors questioned the Albanian identity and coveted its territory. Its people were likely the most maligned in Europe for eschewing civilization alongside their alleged love of violence and barbarity. In this milieu, Zog charted a strange course that in some ways invited both invasion and then the unique form of communism that followed in Albania. So, his story, and that of his son and heir to the throne, Leka I, opens a window onto the world of small-state survival.

* * *

In April 1961, King Zog was in Paris, waiting to die from multiple undisclosed ailments largely caused by a very unhealthy and sedentary lifestyle that apparently included 100 cigarettes a day. By then, he was a joke of sorts and an object of ridicule. For some, he was the original King of Ruritania, or worse, merely a character in Herge's Tin Tin Balkan adventure, *King Ottakar's Sceptre*. He had left a big villa in Cannes on the Riviera to be closer to hospital care and a cemetery plot in the Paris suburbs, not in a grandiose crypt in his homeland that he always hoped would become a staple for school visits and foreign diplomats eager to learn about the first entirely indigenous king of Albania, who fought against all foes to save Albanian independence. The *New York Times* once dubbed him the hardest working monarch in the world, with a claim that he worked 18 hours a day and even got up at 6 am with the eagles. According to lore, the wild eagles, Albania's national symbol, simply came to him. Another reputable paper called him the "Balkan Napoleon," but it was never clear what that really meant. A burial back home, which he so craved, would need to wait until the communists were driven out.

But in 1961, no matter how much he hoped, the end of communism seemed unlikely. He would never get the revenge he felt owed to him and his son. The communists of Albania, and everywhere else in Eastern Europe for that matter, seemed surprisingly resilient. They proved to be even more effective at eliminating opponents than Zog could have ever dreamed. In power since 1944, the communists won two wars—one against the occupation forces of Italy and then Germany, and another more brutal conflict against internal opponents.

After the war, the communists waged yet another war, this time on class enemies. Zog was, at least at the beginning, the foremost class enemy of all: a mountaineer of the former Islamic ruling class who had embraced a ridiculous facsimile of a Western monarchy. Declared a non-person when Albania became not just a republic but a People's Republic in 1945, by 1961 even the communists had nearly forgotten Zog, condemned to Marx's dustbin of history as a feudal reactionary. Zog was not even good enough to be labeled a counter-revolutionary, but just a mere tool of foreign powers and, although never technically a fascist, still an ally of the fascist Benito Mussolini. Certainly, Zog had to wonder whether the communists were right about him. Having dominated Albanian political life from 1920 until 1939, hyperbole aside, much of what the communists said and wrote was true.

Albania was hardly as he left it. Even eight years after Stalin's death in March 1953, it was still run by hard-core Stalinists devoted to a crash program of top-down modernity at any cost. The peasants, well over 80 percent of the country, whom Zog had left landless, poor, and illiterate, were herded onto collective farms, which were only marginally better than Zog's feudalism. The mountaineers of his homeland of Mat were now chanting slogans like "Down with Western Imperialism" or cheering on the one and only communist leader, Enver Hoxha, with shouts of "Long live the party, long live you, Comrade Enver, as long as our mountains" under outsized banners of Marx, Engels, Lenin, and Stalin. In the 1950s, people even named their sons "Marenglen" for Marx, Engels, and Lenin. Zog must have struggled to imagine an uneducated peasantry forced to engage in bizarre ideological battles, learn Marxism-Leninism-Stalinism, and practice class warfare.

The remnants of the Zog-era Tirana elite had been forced out of their two-story Italian-style villas built off the main boulevard. They had bad "political biographies" in communist speak—they needed to be reeducated. Some fled Albania, while others found themselves in internal exile in a remote village without plumbing, or prison or forced labor in a new mine after a show trial. Their stately homes were confiscated and turned over to largely uneducated party loyalists who could not hide their glee at leaving behind a village for a house with indoor plumbing, electricity, a bathtub, and an art collection left behind by the former owners. The communist party bosses eventually settled in an exclusive part of Tirana called the Block, complete with all kinds of amenities, sealed off from the regular people. There, they availed themselves of all the good things in life denied to everyone else. But, by the standards of thievery and kleptocracy in communist Europe, the Albanian communists were somewhat modest, even austere, eschewing jewels and palaces in favor of a few suits, an extra refrigerator, foreign medical services, and lots of food and drink. They never stole as much as Zog.

A school system was created from scratch to create a labor force that could sustain an industrialization drive. The Stalin Textile Mill came and later the Steel of the Party Mill were built so that Albania could be more than an olive grove, electricity was finally brought to the villages, mines were opened and worked by political prisoners, history was re-written as a class struggle, Soviet-style cultural palaces with Soviet money were inaugurated, churches and mosques were closed, and Albania remained the only country in the communist bloc to keep Stalin on the pedestal guiding the country's politics and economics. Heroes one day became traitors the next in a place where the communists turned black into white and back again in an on-off again cycle of violence that kept everyone, even the top party elite, guessing as to what was next. Uncertainty was their forte. As Hoxha's maxim went, class struggle proceeds "in waves and follows a zig-zag course; it rises and subsides, it sharpens and mollifies, but it never stops nor does the flame of the class struggle ever go out."

A one-channel radio, approved and registered, was found in almost every home to get the latest word from the party, which spoke the language of plan targets, new dams, and an undeniably bright future of plenty after the exploiting classes had been completely vanquished. Television came in the 1960s, but there was just one channel that ran for only a few hours a day. In Paris, if Zog flipped through some of the communist newspapers that made it to him in Paris, he would have learned that in 1958 the communists had 627,000 sheep and 1,000 cows artificially inseminated. Zog did get the occasional mention in the party press: satrap, lackey of the imperialists, and a hangman were the most common descriptions. He might have looked through another paper from 1957 telling of the remains of one of the people he had murdered in Italy being returned to Albania for a proper state burial.

Purge after purge, which could send even a top party leader in front of a firing squad or drive one (or even two) to suicide, had put Albania in the hands of a narrow elite, a red aristocracy, who, in 1961, were looking more and more to communist China for inspiration instead of their Soviet masters, who had decided that Stalin was not so great after all. Only communist leader Enver Hoxha, in power since 1944, and his tiny inner circle knew that the Soviet advisors and their military bases would be chucked out to be replaced by Chinese advisors in Mao jackets and buttons. Albania was drifting ever so slowly into the embrace of the People's Republic of China. Who could know then that China would get a beachhead in Europe? Chinese-made trucks would replace Soviet-made ones to ply Albania's few roads, bringing Maoism and terraced agriculture. The Chinese model was pure Stalinism and Albania's Stalinists were becoming Maoists too. School kids would soon turn to Mao's lofty thoughts alongside Stalin's to make them feel good about Albania's communism and the uniqueness of its path to prosperity and modernity. Unlike the capricious Soviets, the Chinese were prepared to not just provide cash for Albania but to allow them to maintain the loving embrace of the Stalinist economic and political model. That mattered most. But a Chinese satellite state in Europe? That was hard to imagine.

In Paris, Zog was obviously running out of cash. The money he looted before he fled Albania was running short. His delegation of followers, the remnants of the royal court, 120 when he fled, was dwindling with fewer and fewer incentives to keep everyone on board. Plus, even to his most loyal, the prospects of a return were obviously increasingly out of the question. Only two real staff members were left in Paris, plus some devotees to the kingdom scattered around the world, working menial jobs largely as airport baggage handlers but with business cards that made them a prince of this or that or a royal plenipotentiary.

Zog stole everything he could carry when he fled on the heels of the Italian invasion in April 1939, but there was only so much one could fit in five cars that were already filled with weapons just in case he had to shoot his way out. Up until then, Italian dictator Benito Mussolini had paid him well to behave, and behave he did. Mussolini's payments to Zog were epic in scale. Zog adored and idolized Mussolini's authoritarian state and his show-manship. Zog called him the Lion. Zog had never been a fascist, as much as he might have wanted to be. He doubted his own people's organizational capacity. He also lacked the patience for ideologies.

Like Mussolini, Zog was a mama's boy with a mother he both loved and feared. Like most dictators, he came from the provinces. As to differences, Zog's father was an Ottoman governor and clan chief. Mussolini's father was a blacksmith who read *Das Kapital* to the young Benito, named after the nineteenth-century liberal president of Mexico. Benito was a commoner, Zog was local royalty. By his own accounts, Mussolini was one of the greatest lovers of the twentieth century. By some accounts, Zog was not, but there were strange rumors that Zog had an affair with his sister, Senije. Zog had no time for paramilitary black or brown shirts; he was just the regular run of the mill dictator that dominated Europe between the wars, dressed in military garb and employing the fascist salute of Mussolini. He was hardly the cruelest person of the era, but he was no sentimentalist either. There was no mass violence. Censorship was an irrelevancy in an illiterate country. He was a replica. Unlike Mussolini, he did not want to save Albania or make it great, respected, and feared. Zog wanted to stay in power and get rich. He was an ordinary tyrant.

Zog lacked Mussolini's curiosity, intellectual depth, and natural charisma. But he shared with Mussolini his suspicion of everyone around him and his fear of rivals. The soft-spoken Zog, who kept his cards close to his chest, had a kind of anti-charisma—more sphinx than lion. His voice was soft, almost inaudible, not prone to bluster or histrionics. Unlike Hitler and Mussolini, grand oratory was beyond him. He never ranted or made use of theatrical gestures or ridiculous poses. He did not study his public performances, as there hardly were any. Unlike most dictators, he did not develop much of a personality cult, and he never projected the idea that he was a man of the people or someone accessible to the masses. He did not wade into crowds but abhorred them. He did not do manual work pitching hay, play with a drugged zoo animal, or swim in frigid waters to show his muscles or manhood. Mussolini got hundreds of letters a day from his adoring citizens while in power. Zog likely got none. Zero. Nobody ever wrote. There is no archive of letters from people for historians to comb for insights. Even Albania's communist leader received thousands upon thousands of letters covering everything from a request for a prison release to permission to seek medical treatment abroad to denouncing a neighbor or a friend.

While Mussolini demanded resources to burnish his own image in film and print and never shut up, Zog loved silence and chose to say almost nothing. But, to his credit, Zog also lacked Mussolini's love of violence. Mussolini sent a million of his own people to early graves, to say nothing of Hitler or Stalin. Zog hardly asked anything of his people, not even blind obedience, just acquiescence to their fate and no resistance.

Zog ran the usual crooked state—more extortion racket than anything else. He outwardly governed by lofty ideals of progress and soft Islam for all, while permitting the worst types of criminals to plunder everything. He spoke the language of modernity, but Zog did not want to build roads, schools, or bridges. Everything was for sale, from a job as a cleaner in a ministry building to a lucrative customs office in a port or a posh diplomatic appointment abroad. Certainly, he admired the faux totalitarianism of Mussolini with its sham "Everything in the State, nothing outside the State, nothing against the State." But Zog understood that that type of control was out of reach for him. This was Albania, not Italy, and these were Albanians, allegedly ungovernable, who recoiled at rules. How could he have known that pernicious control would have to wait for the communists? Hitler's more successful version of totalitarianism just made him envious, but he must have loathed him. Zog surely considered Hitler as ultimately responsible for his life in exile.

While fleecing Italy for millions of lira, Zog stashed some of the stolen cash abroad in foreign banks. His British investment advisors had helped him with investments in the US, Sweden, and Switzerland, but those had since been sold off. The crown jewels were gone too, including the Austrian-made diamond tiara for the royal wedding in 1938. Between leaving Albania in 1939 and arriving in Paris in 1961, there had been stops in Greece, Turkey, Romania, Sweden, France, the United Kingdom for the duration of the Second World War, Egypt under the protection of King Farouk until he was toppled in a revolution, then the Riviera, and, finally, Paris to die. He became a source of information for the US after he got big promises from the CIA to help topple the communists, and in 1951, he bought the 60-room Knollwood Mansion in Muttontown, New York. He paid for it, according to the tabloids, with a bucket of diamonds and rubies because the British would not let him leave England with so much cash. Zog had plans to turn the place into a tiny replica of his Albania, complete with feudal farm and a training ground for an army to invade the "Land of the Eagles" to topple the communists. The Americans later vetoed that idea and the property fell into disrepair and was sold. Zog was stuck in Paris with his wife, the half-American, half-Hungarian minor noble of a long-finished royal line in a country without a king or a queen, the former countess and subsequently Queen Geraldine, his son, Crown Prince Leka, the heir to the throne, his sisters—Adile, Senije, Myzejen, and Maxhide—and his only nephew, Tati, the Prince of Kosovo. Two other sisters had already died: Ruhije in 1948 and Nafije—Tati's mother—in 1955. Both died during Zog's exile in the twilight years of King Farouk's Egypt.

One could presume that Zog's son, Leka, may have wandered around the apartment waving a loaded gun (an indication of an early love of weapons and violence that persisted his whole life) and talking of revenge on the people who robbed them of their kingdom. Getting even was his sole preoccupation. He was the heir apparent for only two days—April 5–7, 1939. He had never really seen Albania, marveled at its ruggedness, the simplicity of life in the mountains of the north or the nearly untouched Adriatic Coast. It is highly unlikely that his father had come clean about the violence that had sustained his rule.

In April 1939, the Italians pragmatically calculated that to maintain respectability and avoid looking weak, they had to invade Albania. Over the course of the previous 16 months, Hitler had eliminated Austria and first taken a chunk and later all of Czechoslovakia; Mussolini felt he had to keep up. The amount of betrayal Zog experienced was typical of the period when Hitler, Mussolini, and Stalin shaped the fate of the world. It was nigh impossible for a small state to survive. Alongside the big players, little people like Zog in Albania, Admiral Miklós Horthy in Hungary, Salazar in Portugal, King Alexander of Yugoslavia, or General Francisco Franco in Spain were

The young Ahmet Zog, undated photo.
Source: Bain News Service, via Wikimedia Commons

the sideshows willing to do pretty much anything to retain power. They invariably took the side of Hitler. Mostly mediocrities in puffed-up military uniforms and thugs who almost never kept their word, the interwar despots ended up with a violent death or exile. Only Franco and Salazar made it through to govern after the Second World War.

Largely uneducated, by the time he was in power Zog spoke Albanian, French, German, and Turkish. His heroes were Gaius Octavius, that is, Augustus of Rome, Napoleon, and, later, Turkey's Mustafa Kemal Atatürk. The little he read about the first two likely confirmed that in two millennia the world had only really changed around the edges. Murder, corruption, extortion, betrayal, exploitation, sex and lies, big and small was all he saw. Most states, he concluded, were just vehicles for the enrichment of a small clique who saw no gains from wealth distribution. Why distribute among 1 million what you could divvy up among 200 people. The cash flowed upward in his Albania, just like everywhere else.

How did it all come to this? King Zog I was born Ahmet Muhtar Bey Zogolli, a Sunni Muslim, in the village of Burgajet, some 60 kilometers northeast of Tirana, as the crow flies, in October 1895. The "Bey" suggested local power in the Ottoman system. Located in what is now northern Albania but was then part of the Ottoman Empire in a region called Mati for the nearby river that flows into the Adriatic, Burgajet was a typical Albanian village of the time. It comprised a collection of homes looking like small towers, with no glass in the windows and no sewage either. Women and men lived largely separate lives, and the home almost always accommodated the livestock on the ground floor. In some cases, the space for people was only separated from the barn by a partition. A large fireplace dominated. The diet was mostly coarse bread. The place had hardly changed in the preceding 500 years, and it would take the communists after the Second World War to bring electricity and some modernity to the place. There were hardly any schools and no roads either. The business of government consisted mostly of bribing local officials. Northern Albania, by all accounts, possessed the last surviving tribal society in Europe in the twentieth century.

The closest town was Burrel, famous for its apples. Later, as king, to provide employment for his tribesmen, who grew violent when restless, Zog would build a prison there for his enemies to have them close and to keep an eye on their visitors too. A visit to a relative there usually ended with an arbitrary arrest. As a prison, Burrel would gain even more renown as the most notorious of almost all prisons in communist Albania, where the politically persecuted would face torture and death. Burgajet had a castle fitting a local leader in the Ottoman Empire, although hardly a castle like Windsor or Balmoral. Later, it was just a ruin, having been purposely abandoned by Albania's communist rulers who demolished it. The peasants of Zog's time eked out an existence growing maize and tobacco and keeping herds of goats. Zogolli's father was an Ottoman governor in the region, a feudal leader of the great Muslim Mati tribe famous for their independence of spirit, or, as the books often described them, "proud mountain folk" who were always well-armed. The Zogolli's were one of four ruling families of the Mat region. Poverty, patriarchy, and blood feud violence defined life. Most men had a better than average chance of dying from blood vengeance than anything like natural causes. Turkish justice was nowhere to be found, so a council of elders decided everything based on the rules set out in a medieval code of customs known as the *Kanun* of Lekë Dukagjini. Sharia or Church law came second to the *Kanun*. In a world of uncertainty, an affront to a man's honor was dangerous, even if it was accidental. A man whose honor had been affronted was socially dead until blood was spilled.

Zog's father was the archetypal big fish in a little pond. His mother, Sadije, a formidable woman by all accounts, was destined to become the queen mother. She doted over her only son the way only an Albanian mother could. Zog's mother had big dreams for her son. The young Ahmet hardly ever spoke. In the Albanian world, all hopes were pinned on the boy to bring honor to the family. This placed enormous pressure on Zog to deliver. The sisters needed only to marry well. Sadije came from one of the region's most famous warlord families, the Toptanis, who were destined to become Zog's enemies too.

Zog was fortunate in that his roots opened many doors to do great things, especially once he decided the pastoral life in the hills or being governor of a small Ottoman province did not appeal. If the Ottoman Empire had survived the First World War, his options were limitless. Likely he would have become a grand vizier (the number two after the sultan). Albanians had long punched above their weight in the world of Ottoman administration because of their fierce loyalty, love of violence, and the fact that unlike many other Balkan peoples subjected to Ottoman rule, most Albanians converted to Islam. After all, Kara Mustafa, an Albanian-born grand vizier in the 1600s, led the great siege of Vienna in 1683. (Though he was subsequently strangled with a silk cord in Belgrade and his head sent to the sultan after he failed to take the city.)

Zog's career in the Balkans was breathtaking in its success—a meteoric rise, as one would say. Partially educated in Constantinople, he fought in the Balkan Wars and the First World War, lived in Vienna for the eclipse of the Habsburg Empire in 1916–1918, and returned to Albania to become the country's youngest cabinet minister at 25, the youngest prime minister at 27, the youngest president at 30, and its first (and only native) king at 33. The papers wrote that Mussolini was Europe's youngest prime minister in 1922, aged 39. Zog had him beat by 12 years. For some, he was a simple criminal who murdered his way to the top; for others, he unified a divided nation and brought stability, if nothing else.

In Paris in April 1961, renewed greatness seemed a long way off. How could Zog know that in nine days he would be dead, almost twenty years to the day after he fled Albania to neighboring Greece for a life of exile and despair? Except for the Greek king, all the other Balkan royalty—Bulgarian, Romanian, and Yugoslav—were driven out by communists. But it would have been worse if Zog had stayed in Albania—the hangman's noose or the firing squad awaited him just as he had shot or hanged his opponents. The communists did not treat their enemies any better than he did, and the cycle of revenge apparently had no end in Albania. He would have ended up like Mussolini—a bloated and savagely beaten corpse hanging upside down alongside his lover in a gas station in Milan. There were no gas stations in Albania. He had seen to that at least.

Twenty-two years in exile was a long time. Stuck in a Paris suburb, in an apartment, a far cry from the chateau on the Riviera, the palace King Farouk of Egypt loaned him in Alexandria, or his palace in the Albanian coastal town of Durres, Zog likely pondered the things people wrote about him and his people. Such a maligned and misunderstood country and people from the very beginning. So "oriental" and "exotic," but only kilometers from Italy and bordering Greece. Newspaper photos always showed him in the garish white military outfit he had designed himself—white hat with white ostrich feathers, white jacket, white pants, white gloves, and white leather boots. Mussolini did worse, Zog must have thought. He wore a yellow tuxedo. And besides, in what became known as the interwar period it was simply *de rigueur* to wear a uniform.

His homeland had been in the hands of the worst type of communists since November 1944; even the Romanians fared better. Enver Hoxha, an upstart pseudo-intellectual from the southern town of Gjirokaster, just one of many dictators that sprang up from the periphery, had taken over. A Muslim like Zog, Hoxha waged his own wars on Albania's three faiths: Islam, Catholicism, and Orthodoxy—breaking Albania's long tradition of religious tolerance by essentially banning all religions. Religion was all but destroyed by the communists. Mosques became movie theatres, and the Catholic leadership was jailed or executed. Zog never did anything on that scale, but he did execute a Catholic priest in 1926 for starting a revolt against his rule. Like Atatürk, the founder of modern Turkey, he only wanted to westernize Albania by limiting the impact of Islam, which he thought detracted from his western veneer. For him, Islam was merely a marker of backwardness. He adored Atatürk for his willingness to try to break Islam's hold on Turkey. But unlike Atatürk, Zog was profoundly lazy.

Zog possibly regretted sending Hoxha on a state scholarship to Montpellier, France where he was able to see, for the first time, just how badly off Zog's Albania was, and he also learned some very basic communist principles that he later used against him. But Hoxha had learned one thing from Zog: kill all the people who helped you get where you are. After he secured power, Hoxha later enticed all Zog's tribal allies to Tirana on the promise of amnesty—and then shot them all.

Zog left Albania almost as he found it. No roads, no trains, no nothing. Uneducated throughout and totally impoverished. To be fair, Zog also started from nothing. Over 500 years of Ottoman rule and nothing beyond mosques, baths, and minarets. Albania, at the end of Zog's reign, would be Europe's last feudal country—a country of big landlords and poor peasants scratching out a living as nothing more than rock farmers.

Albania's north, where Zog came from and which some observers likened to Europe in the twelfth century, was still governed by the *Kanun* of Lekë Dukagjini, a collection of tribal laws largely from the 1400s that guided everything from marriage and property to guests and blood feuds. It was a constitution of sorts. It was the basis of law for a country living on a clan system. It was also a handbook for regulating and even containing blood feuding, which certainly predated the Kanun itself. According to the maxim "blood for blood," only one person could be killed to avenge the blood of another person, and blood could never be unavenged. As such, blood feuds were a feature of Albanian life, and politicians were particularly susceptible to incurring blood even if they merely ordered a murder or sent someone to the gallows. Blood feuds could last for generations. They were almost impossible to end.

The laws of the *Kanun* took precedence over anything from church, mosque, or state. As a ruler, Zog closed the Sharia courts and banned polygamy. Taking a page from the French Revolutionaries after 1789, he took control of religious appointments and the money of churches and mosques as well. Divorce was permitted. He later married a Catholic. To reverse the darkness that held sway in the north, after banning veils and polygamy, Zog sent his sisters on a showy westernization tour with short skirts, white sailor suits, and hats, hoping to convince a cowed and fearful people that the future looked bright as long as they shed Islam and loved their king. Zog was too fearful to head north on his own. If your wife failed to live up to expectations, you could also simply shoot her. As an old saying went, "Even the beams of a house shed tears when a girl is born."

By 1961, the exiled King Zog no longer had visitors. Even those few people who escaped communist Albania, largely by risking their lives swimming to nearby Corfu in Greece, hardly made what had once been a mandatory pilgrimage to see their one and only king. Thus, they could not tell him of the horrors of Albanian communism, with its food shortages, nighttime queues for eggs, nosy neighbors seeking social mobility by denouncing a friend, enemy, or loved one, whispering in cafes, and constant surveillance. Only the odd journalist, doing some pathetic "where are they now" feature, still bothered to visit. One British tabloid, writing about him while in England, remarked that he was "morose, sullen, and bored" and "living in sham pomp."

The newspapers always wrote that he had survived 55 assassination attempts. Zog could only think of two. But he did kill more than 55 people. In fact, Zog murdered all his serious political opponents and often had the murderer of his opponents murdered to further cover his tracks. He likely had his uncle, Esad Pasha Toptani, murdered in Paris in 1920 with a trial that put Albania on the map and set a new standard for international justice. That was a murky affair. The trial had been fantastic, gripping all of France. Then, in 1924, Zog had the person that killed Esad Pasha, 28-year-old Avni Rustemi, killed in turn, just as he was setting off to America, visa in hand, to start a new life with like-minded Albanian emigres in Boston. That was particularly nasty.

Zog never did the killing himself—he was a man who sent emissaries. He ordered the killings of political opponents mostly in cafes, such as Luigj Gurakuqi in 1925 outside a Bari café. As a favor to the Serbs and himself, he murdered pesky Kosovo leaders such as Bajram Curri in the mountains of northern Albania in 1925 and Hasan Bey Prishtina while the latter sipped coffee in Thessaloniki in 1933. He had his brother-in-law, his sister Nafije's husband, Ceno Bey Kryeziu, murdered in a Prague café in 1927, making his sister a very happy widow. She chafed at the arranged marriage and never liked her husband. Zog obviously did not, either. He had to have Ceno Bey's assassin murdered, too, when he started blabbing about Zog's hand in the affair. Strangely, Albania's communist ruler would also have his brother-in-law executed.

There were also those two Americans he mistakenly murdered, tourists looking for fun and adventure in Albania. Robert Coleman and George DeLong, he recalled, were on a road trip in 1924 near the town of Mamuras, not too far from Tirana. But that was a case of mistaken identity; he thought they were officials from the League of Nations. He wanted to create chaos, calls for order, and disgrace his opponents—not cause a scandal that incurred the wrath of the Americans. Things got very ugly. That was a close call. There were others he had since forgotten.

He also had loads of people executed after sham trials for opposing him in various local revolts. There were also the émigré Albanians, often in cahoots with the American or British secret services, whom he helped to send back to Albania to topple the communists in 1949 and after. That was a disaster. Poorly trained, landing by night on the coast or dropped by parachute, and tipped off by spies in the British Secret Service that they were coming, the communists executed them upon arrival. But he was responsible for them being there in the first place. That was another story he surely wanted to set right. It was not really his idea.

Zog pardoned a few people too, thus saving them from the gallows. Foreign diplomats encouraged him to extend such pardons and warned him about incurring too much debt in blood. Of the two assassination attempts, there was that one in the Albanian parliament when Zog was prime minister in 1924. There was also the one in Vienna in 1931, after he was king, when he left the opera in the hope of waving to an adoring crowd of on-lookers but instead almost died in a hail of bullets from people who hated him. Even if he could no longer recall the other 53, it made for a good story, and it was true that he was always armed. Everyone always wrote that. On both occasions he shot back. Everyone wrote that too. A British traveler, Wadham Peacock, remarked that Albanians were good people except for their propensity for homicide.

On the plus side, there was also his remaking of Tirana from a shabby, dusty village of 17,000 people, with one bazaar, houses that looked like cottages, and 140,000 olive trees, into a tiny mock fascist town. For this, he used Mussolini's cash and Italian architects, complete with a grand boulevard for troops to march up and down and buildings adorned with fascist-style soldiers' heads above the doors. He brought a European royal veneer to himself by marrying a half-American, half-Hungarian countess who had fallen on hard times. He tried to save the Jews from Hitler not once but three times. He tried to save Albania from the communists after the war by working with British and American intelligence to foment a revolution in Albania that would, in the hopes of the optimistic planners, act as a catalyst for the collapse of communism in Europe.

He was also a habitual liar. Speaking the truth, especially to foreigners, was a character flaw—a weakness. He was also happy to spread a rumor that he saved Albert Einstein from Hitler's goons, successfully perpetuating a myth that King Zog was a friend to imperiled Jews in the 1930s. He was, quite simply, after cash payments from the Jews which he would have pocketed.

Chapter Two

From Constantinople to Tirana

B urgajet Castle was not as remote as it could get in Albania, but it was close—low mountains that gave way to a far more rugged northern Albania where life had not changed much in 500 or even 1000 years. At that moment in time, the Ottoman Empire controlled vast territories from Yemen to Bosnia. Constantinople fell in 1453 and Athens went five years later and the muezzin's call to prayer replaced church bells. It was no different in Albania, conquered in the late 1300s after being little more than a battleground between Eastern and Western Christianity. Albania merely emerged as the least developed part of the European part of the Empire, where, as rumor had it, only sheep, goats, and fighting men could survive. Albanians may have owed some allegiance to one big family or another, but mostly they owed allegiance to themselves. The Ottomans envisioned something a bit more disciplined with taxes and military service, but fully subduing the Albanians, considering such rugged and inaccessible territory, proved nearly impossible. They were thus largely left alone, which meant progress eluded them. In terms of law, the *Kanun* prevailed for the next 400 years. Albanians never completely settled into their place in the Ottoman Empire and resistance was a normal part of life. But violent retribution was as well. In 1830, 500 Albanian leaders and their guards were invited to a conference where the Ottomans slaughtered them all.

When Zog entered the world in 1895, the Ottoman Empire was arguably dying a slow death—"the sick man of Europe," as the cliché went. Reforms had been tried, but the cause seemed lost. A constitution came and went. The West was meddling in its internal affairs. This was after more than five centuries of breathtaking success in conquering much of the Balkans and later Hungary too. The Europeans were growing impatient with a Muslim power in Europe. As with the Greeks, the West and Russia took up the banner of the persecuted Christians. Holy War was in the air. The Balkan Christians had to be liberated. By 1895, most of Ottoman Europe had been lost in a series of wars as the Ottoman Empire beat a retreat from the Balkans. This left a series of new, largely Christian states that were tiny and aggressive imperialist powers in their own right, seeking Great Power allies in London, Berlin, Moscow, Paris, Rome, and Vienna for grabbing more territory from the Ottomans. The problem was the Albanians were there. While the general Western perception of the Ottoman Empire was that it was a cruel and inhumane enterprise, it never meant sympathy for the mainly Muslim Albanians.

Zog's father died when he was eight, so he hardly knew him. After being home-schooled by his mother, who largely inspired Zog with tales of Albanian greatness in the service of the sultan, in 1907 he was sent to Constantinople as part of an established system that meant sons of governors served in the Ottoman military. He was a hostage of sorts. At twelve years old, Zog found himself destined to be a soldier in the sultan's army. Zog was the first in his family to make the trip to the Ottoman capital, and he did it on horseback with a few very meager possessions, trudging through the villages of the remaining parts of the Ottoman Empire in Europe. The route took him from Burgajet on the edges of the Roman Via Egnatia through the Albanian towns of Tetovo and Skopje in Ottoman Macedonia, through Bulgaria, then Edirne, and on to Constantinople.

Zog was entitled by the standards of the time, but only by the standards of the Balkans in the late nineteenth century. His castle lacked plumbing and life in the Mat region was destitute for most. Things were different in the capital. In Constantinople, he studied at the renowned Galatasaraj High School. Constantinople was a far cry from the mountains of Mati, and Zog found himself in a city for the first time, with its electric lights, streetcars, and constant chatter. Zog got a number of firsts there—his first crack at politics and his first serious role model. Moreover, this would not be the first time Zog would find himself in the midst of an empire on the way out—he would be in Vienna for the twilight of the Habsburg Empire in 1918 and for the end of Egypt's Ali dynasty in 1952.

In 1908, Zog watched an empire change in an instant. Constantinople, a city of democrats and dogs as the locals said, was awash in new flags and calls for a new era of restored constitutionalism that had been abandoned in 1878. The empire's multiple nationalities joined the call for "Justice", "Freedom," "Brotherhood," and "Unity." The Empire got a new parliament of Turks, Arabs, Slavs, Albanians, Armenians, Jews, and Greeks. Faced with the growing challenge of nationalism, the Ottoman Empire was to become a multinational empire to stave off total collapse. But in 1908 there were for sure more dogs than democrats. A group of soldiers, led by Mustafa Kemal, or Atatürk, who would later establish the Turkish Republic after the First World War, instigated the Young Turk Revolution, which overthrew the sultanate of Abdul Hamid II and sent him to house arrest in Thessaloniki and later Constantinople. When the forces of counter-revolution tried to unseat the Young Turks, they marched on the capital, and Zog was there to see just what could happen when disciplined soldiers tried to change the course of history. Abdul Hamid was replaced with his more pliant brother, Mehmed V, who spent his life in near total confinement, deprived of even newspapers to read, or so he said.

Zog was still in Constantinople when the city's governor ordered 80,000 of the dogs deported to the tiny nearby island of Sivriada in the Sea of Marmara, where they all died. Zog learned something from this too. The Albanians, by far the most dependable of the sultan's multinational empire, saw themselves replaced as the palace guards. Inside Albania, Albanians started to demand more language rights. An Albanian nation, hitherto ignored, had to be contended with. The Albanians were in open revolt, but who cared about oppressed Muslims?

Mustafa Kemal must have inspired the young Zog on so many levels. The Young Turks were a loose collection of reformers inside the Ottoman Empire. They were the twentieth-century equivalent of the eighteenth-century French Revolutionaries, especially in attitudes towards religion. Islam, at least for them, was a threat and a vehicle for Arabic influence. It is likely Zog started to question his own Islamic faith and its hold on the Albanians as he began to comprehend how Islam worked against Albanian nationalistic ambitions. Zog was hardly raised a Muslim. Most Albanians had converted to Islam with the Ottoman invasions in the 1300s, but that had been a pragmatic move; it was a way to keep the peace, reduce taxes, and achieve upward mobility, which many did. For most of the time, the Ottomans left the Albanians alone if they paid their tributes, sent their sons as hostages, and provided troops when required. The warlike Albanians, especially in the north, embraced the Ottoman military state with ease, while the southerners, often Christians, chafed at living in a theocratic state. If in Greece the Ottomans found antiquities, honey, and olive oil, in Albania they found their most devoted soldiers. The Albanians who stayed as Christians, either Catholic or Orthodox, faced marginalization and many chose emigration. In the Ottoman Empire, nobody came knocking at the door to demand conversion.

The promise of a new Ottoman Empire, even a cosmopolitan one, inspired some Albanians who saw in the Young Turks a way ahead that would give the nascent Albanian national idea support—especially since the Ottoman Empire had banned Albanian-language education and publishing in 1902. Albania and Albanians played a fundamental role in the events of the 1908 Young Turk revolution. While many Albanians supported Sultan Abdülhamid—especially the Albanian troops who served in his palace guard—many took part in the revolution against his rule, and one of its leaders was an ethnic Albanian.

Until then, in the European capitals that mattered, the Albanians were an afterthought. The great unifier of Germany, Otto von Bismarck, once remarked that "there was no such thing as an Albanian nationality." By 1908, in the Balkans, the Greeks, Serbs, Montenegrins, Romanians, and Bulgarians all had a state. The problem was they all wanted a bigger one. They all had their patrons too. The Albanians, with their largely illiterate people and three religions, faced assimilation, deportation or extinction if the national expansion projects of the Serbs, Montenegrins, or Greeks won out. At the beginning, the Young Turks promised the Albanians a space, or more precisely, a fiefdom, where they might flourish, and they embraced it, Zog especially. It was a start. The Young Turk revolution gave rise to an entirely new Albanian national movement.

Zog then may have started to buy into the idea of an Albania rooted in the West, like Greece, even though the Renaissance and Enlightenment had bypassed Albanian territory almost completely. While the new Young Turk government restored the defunct constitutional order, they later changed course. Decentralization and tolerance for the multinational project gave way to centralization and the triumph of an Ottoman identity, leaving the Albanians high and dry. Zog and others were betrayed. The Albanians would have to wait for another moment to realize their national dreams.

Zog's first foray into Albanian nationalism expanded his circle of friends. In Constantinople, Zog may have encountered his uncle on his mother's side, Esad Pasha Toptani. Likely born in Tirana in 1863, Esad was one of the most dangerous, selfish, and cruel individuals in the Ottoman Balkans prior to his assassination in Paris in 1920. In addition to being a wealthy landlord and racketeer who shook down the peasants for their crops, he was also the archetypal traitor, an inveterate liar, and one of the real gangsters that made their fortunes in the dying days of the empire and in the promise of the new Albanian state that came out of it. Unscrupulous, he had more blood on his hands than most and a violent death for him was simply inevitable. He was simply born to be executed. In 1908, he was one of the many Albanians charged with protecting the sultan and propping up a decrepit empire. Everyone in Constantinople knew him for that and for the sheer charisma of his personality. Esad's propensity for violence was already well known. When his brother was killed by one of the sultan's men, he killed the assassin on Constantinople's Galata Bridge in broad daylight.

In 1908, Esad felt he knew which way the wind was blowing and joined the Young Turks, especially since the sultan had ordered his brother's murder. For him, the move towards a kind of autonomy for Albanian lands in the empire would put him in power. He was an unscrupulous opportunist destined to wreak havoc on the Albanian national dream. Esad did not dream big, but small—just a tiny Muslim fiefdom was all he wanted.

The 13-year-old Zog, like many Albanians in the Ottoman regime, also grabbed the nationalism that came with the Young Turks, hoping that it would open possibilities for an eventual Albanian state. The Albanians were to be disappointed. The Young Turks eventually walked away from the empowerment of the nationalities in the empire, a change which later morphed into the violence that shaped Young Turk national policy towards the Armenians and others during the First World War. The Albanians got increasingly demanding and subsequently faced a crackdown, but not a genocide, in the form of new taxes, reduced rights, mandatory conscription, and, most annoyingly, attempts to disarm them. The Albanians needed a patron, but in the hierarchy of nations no one had ever even heard of them. The Greeks had the British and the Russians, the French defended the Serbs, but who was defending Muslim Albanian interests?

Zog stayed in the Ottoman capital until 1912. His fortunes changed with a series of brutal wars in the Balkans that provided Europe's first real experience with ethnic cleansing. They also constituted a dress rehearsal for the First World War and the subsequent end of Ottoman rule in Europe and the emergence of something totally unexpected: the birth of a somewhat independent Albania. Zog was there.

Chapter Three

From Shkoder to Sarajevo

A map of the Balkans in 1912 shows that the shrinking Ottoman Empire held on to very little of what had once been significant territory in Europe. Only Albania and Macedonia were left as spoils, and Bulgarians, Greeks, Montenegrins, and Serbs had a historic claim to the very same territory. Each claim was iron-clad in its veracity in terms of owning the past. It would take three wars to settle the disputes.

By January 1912, the new Ottoman government had embraced a policy of Ottomanization—which meant Turkification—which foretold disaster for the little peoples of the Balkans. The Albanians stopped paying taxes and threatened to have the tax collectors murdered. A sensationalist media alleged that Ottoman troops brought in cholera in hopes of decimating the Albanians. But at the same time, the Ottoman Empire distributed guns to Albanian Muslims to defend themselves from their Christian neighbors. Cash went to warlords. Random Christian paramilitaries (and Muslim ones too) roamed Albania, Kosovo, and Macedonia, slaughtering villagers. Anarchy reigned in what was called European Turkey. Greeks, Serbs, and Montenegrins probed into Albanian space with extreme violence. The West easily bought the prevailing Christian narrative: the Muslims had to pay for Ottoman misrule.

The two Balkan Wars of 1912 and 1913 were nasty affairs that were a harbinger of what twentieth-century warfare was to become. In the first conflict, which began in the fall of 1912, Montenegro launched a series of attacks to end the Ottoman presence in Europe, with a focus on northern Albania and the town of Shkoder. The Albanians were in the way. The Christian powers set aside their differences to remake the Balkans in their favor.

Led by the Montenegrin King Nikola Petrović, who would end up in exile long before Zog, the Montenegrins sought Shkoder—the ancient seat of Montenegrin kings, according to Nikola. This was untrue, but that hardly mattered. When he was not dreaming of a Greater Montenegro at the expense of the Albanians, Nikola racked up massive gambling debts that forced him to ask the Russians or the Austrians to cover them in exchange for loyalty. He had big dreams too, such as draining Lake Shkoder to make more arable land.

Bulgaria, Greece, and Serbia declared solidarity with Montenegro. The so-called Balkan League was a bit of a surprise as the Great Powers never caught wind of what the four Balkan states were planning together, since nobody could ever imagine the four of them cooperating. What was most astonishing was just how many troops the Balkan states were able to mobilize—over 700,000. There were more volunteers than spaces as the war spirit was everywhere, a spirit that would be recreated elsewhere in Europe in July 1914. The goal was simple: to get the Muslims out of Europe and liberate their Christian brethren. Far outnumbering the Ottoman army, the Balkan allies won easily before quarreling over the territorial spoils in the Second Balkan War. Bulgaria, not satisfied with its gains from the First Balkan War, turned on its one-time allies, Serbia and Greece, eventually leading Romania and the Ottoman Empire to seize Bulgarian territory in turn. Christian solidarity had its limits.

Zog fought wherever he could but mostly in the north of Albania, where he engaged largely against Montenegrin invaders alongside Ottoman forces. He also returned to his native Mati valley to save it from the invading Serbs. Zog earned a reputation as a fierce warrior, something he embellished over time, but he also earned his stripes as the consummate intriguer. In any case, the Serb army marched into Albania with incredible cruelty, hoping to completely exterminate the Muslim Albanians and convert the Catholic ones by force. As religion hardly had any hold on the Albanians, many converted willingly in hopes of being on the winning side or simply to stay alive. Arriving in a village, the Serbs set fire to all the homes and shot everyone in sight. The rampage was repeated elsewhere. Women and children were never spared. The journalists covering the war agreed it was not warfare but slaughter. Zog had a bird's-eye view of the carnage. The Serbs boasted of passing the Albanians "under the sword" and massacring entire tribes. In one village, the Serbian army led all married men outside of the village before ransoming them back to their wives. When the wives paid for their husbands' freedom, however, the men were locked into a mosque instead and killed by shelling. Those who were unable to escape and spared the death penalty were forcibly assimilated by the conquering armies.

It was no better in the south. For many Greeks, if you were Orthodox, you simply had to be Greek, even if you were Albanian. The Greeks were in expansionist mode and bent on establishing the Greece of the Five Seas (the Ionian, Aegean, Marmara, Black, and Libyan Seas). The Greeks, like the Serbs, did their best to further the claim that Albanians were simple savages. Traveling with the Greek army was an American captain who claimed that Albanians were not a nation but a geographic location—a group of heathens who earned a living by stealing other people's sheep.

The incredibly bloody Balkan Wars, in their own way, opened possibilities for Albanians like Esad Pasha and Zog, but it could have just as easily gone the other way. These wars gave the twentieth century its first taste of ethnic cleansing, as everyone sought not just territory but homogeneity too. Muslims, and that included most of the Albanians, had to go. It was not just army against army, but neighbor against neighbor too. The Turks had to be driven out, as the then president of the University of California, Dr. Benjamin Ide Wheeler, said, calling for "swords to be drawn, streaming blood red" if necessary to end "the fatalism of the Orient." A people and a way of life had to be eliminated.

These wars were the twentieth century's first great cataclysm, where regular and irregular armies, filled with an unprecedented number of eager conscripts, engaged in massive atrocities in regions that the Ottomans had largely left ungoverned. The people of the Balkans suffered immensely from 1912 until 1913 in the span of the two Balkan wars, but undoubtedly Muslims fared the worst when nations and religions went to war for ethnic purity. For some, it was a holy war of "cross against crescent," which was made clear especially by the Bulgarian king, Ferdinand, who explicitly called for such.

Each army, whether Greek, Serbian, Montenegrin, Bulgarian, or Ottoman, had the goal of completely removing the population and its way of life from the lands which it conquered—the Albanians were caught in the middle. By the Second Balkan War the former allies had completely dehumanized themselves when Bulgaria turned on its one-time allies. The national presses depicted their enemies as inhuman monsters; war and the violent annihilation of them was the order of the day. The fear that it would cause a wider European war was never far from people's minds, which probably explains the haste with which the Great Powers intervened to settle the Albanian question.

Ultimately, the war's impact on the Balkan's Muslim peoples was extermination, emigration, or forced assimilation. Extermination, meaning the murder and destruction of entire populations and villages, occurred systematically and was perpetrated by each army. Upon entering a Muslim village, local Muslims were disarmed, with some being killed indiscriminately. Survivors were ordered to stay inside under penalty of death, waiting for their turn to be brought before a commission. In some places, according to reports, the trial they faced was simple, with only one question put to the judges: "Is he good or is he bad?" One vote was enough to condemn a person to death. The extermination of an alien population was at the heart of it all. Brought to its envisioned conclusion, a Balkans without Muslims was possible. Ottoman forces responded in kind and burned Greek villages and Greeks forces burned Muslim villages. Revenge and reprisals, based on lurid reports in the newspapers of the day, created a frenzy of violence and bloodletting. In the European capitals, the Balkans as a place of savagery took hold. Ottoman forces routinely captured a town's notables, executed them, and then decapitated them as well. Turks in Bulgaria were massacred, with bodies piled in the streets. Rumors again spread that Turkish physicians headed into battle with typhus and cholera microbes.

Covering the Balkan Wars as a journalist was Leon Trotsky, writing for a Kyiv paper starting in September 1912. Ultimately there to make a living, he wrote under the pen name Antid Oto from the word "antidote." Even Trotsky, who would go on to initiate and preside over so much bloodshed, was utterly stunned by the violence of the Bulgarian armies in particular. No doubt it inspired him, as Trotsky later acknowledged he learned quite a bit in the Balkans, claiming it prepared him to take over the Red Army in 1918.

The Muslim Albanians got lumped in with the Turks. All the religious tropes came out. The war would end oriental despotism. It gave Christians the opportunity to get back at their Muslim neighbors and landlords, to exact revenge, and to act on existing grudges.

Given the way things generally went for Muslims in the Balkans, the First Balkan War could have easily meant the near total disappearance of the Albanians. In Kosovo, especially, which the Serbs gained in the war, Albanians were subject to the worst type of violence with the aim of completely altering the ethnic character of the region. The Serbs and others later denied the atrocities, claiming the tolerance of their rule and even proclaiming that the Jews had also found their promised land in Serbia.

But in November 1912, faced with extinction, the 17-year-old Zog now found himself alongside Esad Pasha and other patriots raising the Albanian flag in the coastal town of Vlora and declaring independence and hoping for the best. Ismail Qemal bey Vlora, a one-time senior official in the Ottoman Empire, called on the Great Powers for help. Eager to please, in a letter to the European powers that mattered, the Albanians acknowledged their savagery and ever so politely requested to join civilized Europe. (They have been asking ever since.) The powers said fine, accepted the burden of the civilizational role, and even later acknowledged that the Balkan Wars were partly their fault for failing to civilize the Balkans in the first place. All the Albanians needed in 1912 was a sponsor.

If luck had evaded the Albanians during 500 years of Ottoman rule, things looked a bit rosier in 1912. The Albanians did have sponsors—the Habsburg Empire and even Italy—but both for deeply cynical reasons. The Austrians had long been taking the Albanian side; indeed, they had even been building the Albanian nation from scratch for deeply political reasons— to keep Serbia off the Adriatic and the Montenegrins out of Shkoder. They taught the Albanian language in Graz and Vienna, sent nurses and doctors

CHAPTER THREE

to Albania's rugged north, and provided schools. Most Albanians dreamed of being "civilized" by rule from Vienna. Albania's tiny elite begged to be made an Austrian protectorate. By December 1912, the Great Powers decided Albania should be an independent state and set about making borders in an extremely haphazard way. In 1913, in what was the last time the world's powers were able to cooperate before the First World War brought everything crashing down, Austria, with the support of Italy, successfully created the tiny state of Albania out of the remnants of the European part of the Ottoman Empire. Albania's borders were destined to create trouble later on, as they left almost as many Albanians outside the new state as in.

It was a huge foreign policy triumph for the Habsburg Empire. Vienna in 1913 was awash in all things Albanian, especially the Albanian flag—the black, double-headed eagle on a red background was everywhere on the Ringstrasse. For a brief moment, the Albanians mattered, thanks to Austria. The Austrians had stuck it to the troublesome Serbs by making the state of Albania, blocking their dreams of access to the Adriatic Sea. That a bigger war was avoided, or at least postponed until the summer of 1914, was a major miracle as things could have just as easily spun out of control in 1913 as they did later in 1914. The Albanians now had a state but one that was much smaller than they had hoped. Kosovo, even though it possessed a majority Muslim Albanian population, was handed over to Serbia. For the Serbs, a Serbia without Kosovo was unthinkable. Great battles had been lost there and the Orthodox monasteries, dating to the fourteenth century, were national treasures. The Albanians just happened to live there. That was easy to fix with the right amount of violence. The Ottoman Empire ceased to exist in the Balkans. The diplomats who gathered in London in 1913 also agreed to create an Albanian kingdom; they just needed a king. There was lots of interest, especially from Germans.

In the latter part of the nineteenth century, as new Balkan states appeared, Germans were usually sent to become new kings. German kings made sense. After the unification of Germany in 1871, there were loads of dynasties without any role. The Great Powers went to them especially since it was assumed they would be easy to manipulate. Even before Germany became a unified state, there was the young Otto of the Bavarian Wittelsbach family, sent to Greece in 1833. Later, Romania got the German Hohenzollern-Sigmaringens, and Bulgaria got the German Battenbergs, and later the equally German House of Saxe-Cobourg and Gotha. The Serbs had their own dynasties –three in fact—the Petrovićs in Montenegro and the Karadordevićs and Obrenovićs in Serbia. The latter two had fought it out for control of Serbia. The Obrenović dynasty was eliminated in Belgrade in a night of horrible violence in June 1903 when King Alexander and Queen Draga were slaughtered inside their palace by plotters determined to eliminate the Obrenović line completely. Petar Karadordević returned from Swiss exile to rule Serbia. That family would hang around until the communists sent them packing.

As nobody had started hating the Germans yet, the Great Powers, with Austrian prodding and much lobbying by his aunt Elisabeth, who was Queen of Romania, chose the harmless 37-year-old Wilhelm of Wied to become Albania's new king. He came from the minor German principality of Neu-Weid. He was apparently well-connected. He was second cousin to Wilhelm II, the German emperor, and had an aunt who was a princess of the Netherlands.. Visiting his other aunt in Romania gave him experience of Balkan politics. He loved science too, and he had an uncle who had discovered some hitherto unknown Brazilian animals. His wife, Princess Sophie of Schönburg-Waldenburg in Saxony, came from Romania and was allegedly linked to former rulers of the Byzantine Empire. She was a wonderful pianist and harpist who loved strolling through the Carpathian Mountains where she communed with nature daily. In Albania, she claimed that she was to train Albanian women of noble birth to become maids of honor. Mindful of taking over a majority Muslim country, these noble maids would be veiled, with only Wied allowed to look at them.

It was telling that the poor Albanians had to settle for a total nobody who had so little cash too. The Greeks got the son of Bavaria's King Ludwig who financed a new palace in Athens. Wied would offer no such grand interventions, but to be fair, his time was short. By all accounts, he was an incompetent fool. There were other contenders for the Albanian throne, to be sure; a Turk was suggested as Albanians were Muslims, and the British MP, aristocrat, and Albanophile Aubrey Herbert was canvassed too, as he had steadfastly supported the Albanian cause. Apparently only German Kaiser Wilhelm II opposed Wied's appointment by stating the obvious: Wied knew nothing about Balkan politics despite visiting his aunt in Romania. In fact, he had no political experience at all. But in 1913, that hardly mattered. The first king of Greece arrived there when he was only 17 years old. You could learn on the job, apparently. But Wied was a place holder. Nobody expected him to stay for long. The Albanians had long ago been deemed hopelessly ungovernable.

Zog's uncle, Esad Pasha, fresh off ordering the assassination of one of his key opponents in Shkoder who had opposed his sale of the town to the Montenegrin army, was selected to travel to Neuwied Castle to offer the throne to Wilhelm in February 1914. This was somewhat ironic, as Esad was furious that he was not made king himself and that the Great Powers had sent a Christian monarch instead. But he played along. Esad had never left what was the Ottoman Empire, and the visit to the German Empire transformed him the way Zog would later be transformed by his first visit to Vienna. En route to Germany, Esad stopped in Vienna, where he received the Grand Cross of the Order of Franz Joseph I. He was a player who had achieved international recognition. He decided he liked the West—almost too much—and his love of the lavish lifestyle would later send him back there on a one-way journey. When Wied and Sophie arrived in the port of Durres in March 1914, Pasha was there. Wied must have begged the Great Powers to allow him to recreate the pomp and pageantry of February 1833, when the young King Otto arrived in Greece with 70 ships from multiple countries firing cannons as he was awaited by countless delegations. He doubtlessly thought that the Athens of 1833 did not look all that different from the port of Durres. But Balkan state and nation building had lost its veneer, and the Great Powers were fatigued by all these silly problems in the Balkans. Albania was an afterthought once again, but now with a third-tier king. Wied arrived on a single ship on loan from the Italian government and had to recruit locally for staff.

It was still a perfectly colonial moment. The *New York Times* claimed the unfortunate place had only produced hardships, dangers, and troubles. Could a German king subdue the unruly mountain tribes and clans and bring discipline? Could he get the tax-averse Albanians to pay up and give up their addiction to fighting? The cliché of the time—*pays balkanique, pays volcanique*—guided policy. No decision-maker could see Albania as European anyway, so the whole enterprise was colonial but in a European space. Would not a Muslim king have made more sense? Nobody asked such questions. The die was cast in the nineteenth century.

Wied arrived dressed in a blue and grey uniform looking like a man who meant business, and that meant the iron hand for rule breakers, which, according to international observers, was just what the locals wanted anyhow. Upon his arrival, Wied made his first of many huge blunders by making Esad Pasha an Albanian general and minister of the interior. The papers reported he said little upon arrival and, hoping to justify his eerie silence, the papers claimed Wied thus resembled his ancestor, William the Silent of Orange. The scene had a comic opera feel to it—men in showy costumes with big hats and feathers. There was not a long procession as Durres had only one road that functioned and even it was less than a kilometer in length. The town had fallen on hard times since the Romans left, and a nearby amphitheater from the second century had long been covered over by the Ottomans and would have to wait until the 1960s to be discovered again. There were a few scattered buildings near the pier and the minaret of the 400-year-old Fatih Mosque in the distance. The local men sat nearby, smoking and drinking coffee, bewildered by the odd procession. There were no women in sight, recalling the Çajupi poem that best captured the outsized role of women in Balkan life:

> *Men in the shade, playing, discussing, not caring at all that they live because of the wives! Women working in fields, women working in vineyards, the woman harvests the hay, she works day and night.*

There was not much alcohol in Albania in those days. Coffee vendors wandered the streets and scraped the walls with a tuning fork to announce their arrival. A 12-year-old boy sold flatbread from a tin tray. Oddly enough, the new queen addressed the assembled Albanians in French, as she heard the crowd did not speak German. Wied and his wife did not look any more ridiculous arriving in Durres in 1914 with an ostrich feather hat surrounded by dignitaries than the Archduke Ferdinand did three months later in Sarajevo in June 1914.

At that moment, Zog was sidelined, and he watched the spectacle from the periphery. Esad was in the ascendant, controlling the armed Albanians as minister of the interior and taking advantage of a pliant German king who did not have the faintest idea what lay ahead. As expected, Wied did not last long. His wife had to be sedated to get off the ship in the first place and she hated the food. Boiled mutton was not Wied's thing, either. The Greeks refused to recognize Albania's new borders and insisted on fomenting trouble in the country's south where they continued to eradicate the Albanians. Of limited intelligence, Wied got bad advice from everyone and squandered the cash given to him, paying off warlords to avoid rebellions. It was a familiar story. Esad intrigued and plotted insurrection and likely planned Wied's murder. He also took cash, especially from the Italians, to provoke trouble. But someone else decided that murdering a European monarch would invite a cataclysm and got there before Esad could. On June 28, 1914, Gavrilo Princip shot the Habsburg Archduke Franz Ferdinand and his wife Sophie in Sarajevo, and four weeks later the world got the war many people, most of them men, wanted.

Poor Albania was about to disappear hardly a year into its existence. Wied and his wife fled Albania and went to Serbia to make a last stand that amounted to nothing. He never returned to Albania and later refashioned himself as a Nazi when the time was right. Albania disappeared from the map in 1914, overrun by armies from Greece and Serbia. That Albania would appear again as a state was far from assured. Esad and Zog found themselves on opposite sides of the First World War—Esad Pasha joined the Serb cause in the war, attempting to carve out his Muslim fiefdom in the middle of Albania under Serbian auspices once again. Zog decided to fight on the side of Austria-Hungary, and so did another key figure in the future Balkans, Josip Broz, aka Tito, the future dictator of the Yugoslavia that emerged after the Second World War.

Albania's fate as a nation was made even more questionable when the Italians joined the war in 1915. Their price, in the form of a secret treaty, was most of Albanian territory among other things. Thankfully, when the Bolsheviks took power in October 1917, Leon Trotsky took center stage as the new Soviet foreign minister and was kind enough to publish all the secret treaties, and thus likely saved Albania from being swallowed by Italy. But what decided things in what was once Albania was less the number of troops than who could bribe the most. And for much of the war, the Austrians had the most gold to bribe Albania's warlords. However, Zog's ambitions were too much for the Austrians, so they interned him in splendor in Vienna for the duration of the war. The Vienna in which Zog arrived in 1916 was a far cry from the Vienna of the *Grunderzeit*. Zog arrived just in time for the coronation of Charles I, the last Habsburg emperor. The city that had given birth to European modernity—the Vienna of Gustav Klimt, Egon Schiele, Adolf Loos, Sigmund Freud, Gustav Mahler, and Otto Wagner—was shifting to a darker and more brooding side, where one could find Leon Trotsky, Joseph Stalin, Josip Broz Tito, and Adolf Hitler.

In 1917, nobody had ever heard of Zog or even Hitler, Mussolini, Stalin, or Trotsky. The Ringstrasse still had its charm and, to some observers, Zog must have been taken in by the grandeur of it all—neo-renaissance opera, classical parliament, and gothic city hall. Zog probably loved the Ringstrasse, the grand circular boulevard that Franz Joseph I had ordered built to showcase everything that was great about Austrian history. Over and over again, maybe the 22-year-old future king Zog rode the ring tram that circled it.

These were the last days of old Europe—the Europe of Stefan Zweig's cosmopolitan life was dying, but hardly anybody knew what lay ahead, thus confirming that really bad things happen slowly. Vienna would not give art and light but rather give birth to far more sinister ideas that lurked there. Zog arrived too late for the death of Franz Joseph I in 1916, Habsburg emperor since 1848. Franz Joseph started the war in 1914, determined to end what his inner circle referred to as a "foul peace." A short war would be good to clear the air. It had to be short—who could imagine how a then 84-year-old man would even think that the war could last more than a few months. Vienna in 1917 had not recovered from the death of Franz Joseph but the war had to go on. Zog's love of Austria would cause trouble later. Zog stayed almost two years—long enough to see the end of the war, the end of the Habsburg Empire, and the birth of a group of hostile nation states in its place.

Zog's sojourn in Vienna was required because the Habsburgs feared him and his ambitions. If Albania was to reappear after the war, they wanted to control it, and Zog needed to be brought in line before being sent back as an Austrian stooge. This was not the first time Zog would be bought off by a Great Power. In 1917, all the great Albanian families were in Vienna—70 clan chiefs in all—as the Austrians still dreamed of controlling a post-war Albania. Zog was there representing his Mati tribe. Zog was different than the other clan chiefs. The others dressed in national costumes—white fez-like hats, white trousers and beautifully embroidered vests. Zog preferred tailor-made suits and the ever-present cigarette in a holder. The other Albanians there were mostly from Kosovo. Staunchly anti-Serb, these men were beyond the school of hard knocks. Leaders like Bajram Curri and Hasan Prishtina sought a Kosovo free of Serbs and joined with Albania. Curri came from Gjakova in Kosovo and by 1917 had already become known as one of the best Albanian guerilla commanders fighting the Serbs. Prishtina also came from Kosovo, from the rough and tumble region of Drenica, and he too was at the forefront of the war against Serbian control of Kosovo. His dream, at least in his words, was to furrow Kosovo's fields with the bones of dead Serbs. For the Serbs, though, a Serbia without Kosovo was unthinkable. Albanian Kosovar leaders chastised Zog for his lack of zeal for their cause. Zog hated them.

The First World War, set up to save the Habsburg Empire largely from the troublesome Serbs, instead destroyed it in 1918, and with it went their dreams of an Austrian-controlled Albania. Zog left Vienna and returned to Albania in 1919, where he headed into politics full-time, now without his Vienna benefactors. With his personal army of Mati tribesmen, he had to be listened to. He was there for the big events of the day, but his road to power and monarchy was seemingly blocked by his uncle, Esad Pasha Toptani. The Balkan and First World Wars made Toptani filthy rich, emerging as the wealthiest and greediest warlord of the day, having sold out to anyone who would pay him.

In the Albania of 1919, things were different than in the rest of Europe, where the specter of Bolshevism played out in nasty ways. In Hungary, communists seized power for a very bloody 133 days, which led to an even bloodier "White" reaction in its aftermath. In Catholic Bavaria revolution came too, something a young Adolf Hitler witnessed and never forgot. Zog, however, was most fascinated with the events unfolding in Italy where Italians found themselves on the winning side of the war but little to show for it in the subsequent peace treaties. The one-time socialist, schoolteacher, journalist, and full-time schoolyard bully Benito Mussolini launched a new movement to sweep away the old order with cash from the very people who built the old order. With fascist party card number one, Mussolini blended left and right, made violence mainstream, and destroyed his opponents. Mussolini was in some ways the most ordinary of tyrants, a man who spoke for the people with money and the people without money. But in Albania, which was neither a winner nor a loser in the war, calm prevailed as the peasants could hardly make sense of a new world order shaped by fights between the extreme left and extreme right in a place where there was neither left nor right, a working class, a university, or a library.

But it was not in Tirana or Rome but at the Peace Conference in Paris that the fate of Albania and much of the world was being decided in the aftermath of the war. Among the delegates, Esad was considered the Albanian representative. Back home, he could still command 20,000 soldiers if not more. For bizarre reasons, Esad was deemed by the Great Powers to be one of the potential representatives of the new Albanian state, despite his treachery during the war. In Paris since the Peace Conference started in 1919, Esad and his entourage lived a life of total luxury gambling, and buying influence.

The statesmen of the day were making big decisions for the fate of Europe's little peoples. New maps needed to be drawn by people who had never been east of Vienna. The Habsburgs were gone, as were the Romanovs of Russia and the Emperor of Germany too. Only the Ottoman sultan, Mehmed VI, was left on his throne, but he would be gone by 1922, forced out by Atatürk's nationalists, having been condemned and stripped of his titles. He later left Constantinople as an ordinary citizen on board the British warship *Malaya*, which carried him to a life of exile in Malta then Italy. Albania disappeared and its reappearance on the map of Europe was by no means assured at the Paris talks. As in 1912, the Serbs, Greeks, and Italians staked their claims based on bad history and simple racism. Territory was up for grabs again in Europe and the Middle East as the big and little peoples of the world looked for justice and land. Everyone had an ethnic map with maximalist claims, scientific proof from dubious archaeology that they were there first, and suitcases full of grievances.

The Albanians were again in a very weak position. But history was on their side. As descendants of the Illyrians, they were therefore the Balkans' first inhabitants, even before the classical Greeks. The Serbs, who had suffered enormous losses during the First World War, were the darlings of the Peace Conference in Paris, which ensured Esad Pasha was also a darling. With the destruction of the Habsburg Empire, the Serbs joined up with the Croats and the Slovenes to form a new, largely Serb-run kingdom under the Karađorđević dynasty, known as the Kingdom of Serbs, Croats, and Slovenes. It would become the first Yugoslavia in 1929. It again included the Albanian-majority province of Kosovo, which had been won in the Balkan Wars. The Albanians were not happy but what could they do? Esad sought his tiny Islamic emirate as a transit point with lucrative customs posts, shady borders, piracy, kidnapping, arms and drug smuggling, and transit fees—a nice grey zone. Just what the Balkans needed.

Chapter Four

The Killings Begin

In 1920, Albania was a graveyard of failed civilizations—6000 years of them, at least according to Zog—Illyrian, Hellenic, Roman, Venetian, and finally Ottoman. But there was nothing to show for it. At least according to the *civilized* West, Albania was a lesser civilization that required foreign care for its colorful but extremely dangerous people. The dusty and dirty town of Tirana, with only 2,000 mostly Muslim inhabitants, had replaced the port city of Durres as its capital. With its mix of churches, some from the fourth century, and Ottoman-era mosques and the smell of mutton fat and donkey manure, it was hardly on the Grand Tour of European notables. Only one horse-drawn railway line, built by the Austrians during the war with one single car and looking more like a trolley, functioned between Tirana and Durres. Tirana had but one market selling tinware and pots. Donkeys carried wood for sale. A few cafes offered outside seats. Men wore white fezzes, colorful vests, baggy pants, and opinga shoes of leather and wool strips worn by the Albanians for centuries. Men wearing national costume was common. The women dressed mostly in black. The most famous building, the mosque of Suleyman Pasha, built in the 1600s as the first mosque in Tirana, was the center of the town. The Mosque of Et'hem Bey from the 1700s was there too, as was the nearby clock tower from the 1800s. Two Ottoman minarets dominated the modest skyline. There were eight mosques in total. Homes were all one story. After his stint in Vienna, Zog was certain he wanted Tirana to be a European capital—the Ottomans had built a few nice bridges and mosques but not much else. Infrastructure was not their thing. There were no paved roads. The Ottoman impact was limited to food and attitudes. In the 1920s, however, Italian money would transform Tirana from a village into a town. The Tirana that Zog returned to was a Tirana later remade by the Italians who imposed their colonial vision with a single grand boulevard. Zog would later name it after himself, of course, as Zog the First Boulevard and use it for parades which he could watch strategically from afar. The plan was to create a monumental city on a small scale, one that could shed its oriental past. The central square was lined with a few hostile-looking fascist government buildings to house various ministries. The Italians would build a national bank too. The grand boulevard was so out of place in the town that one French architect remarked that he saw a boulevard without a city. This was true. In keeping with the times, the boulevard was later re-named after the Italian King, Victor Emmanuel III, when the time came. The communists would rename it too. The post-communists would continue the same tradition.

The Italians at least allowed the city's main square to be named after Skanderbeg, the Albanian national hero who took on the Ottomans in the 1400s. Skanderbeg fought for an independent Albania of sorts in what was ultimately a "cross against crescent" battle characteristic of the resistance the Balkan peoples offered against the Muslim Ottomans.

A true testimony to the uniqueness of the Albanians was that a majority-Muslim country would choose a Christian who chose to fight Muslims as its national hero. With Italian cash, Zog would later build a palace in Tirana, on Elbasan Street, with a nice house for his mother who doubled as the cook and royal food taster. Food would come from his mother's nearby villa in a locked box escorted by a royal guard at least until she died in 1934. He added another rather grand palace in Durres which he hardly ever visited.

In the Tirana of 1920, with his mother and sisters, Zog's star was on the rise and his family could not wait to start climbing a social ladder that he could fashion from scratch. Given that he had his own army of Mati tribesmen, he was accordingly made minister of the interior in Albania's first post-war government. But there was a rival government, maybe even three. Esad Pasha was still in Paris, tooting his horn and spending big in an effort to challenge the legitimacy of the new government in Tirana. The French and Serbs wanted him back in Tirana. By then, given his performance in the First Balkan War and the First World War, Zog's status as a warrior was fixed. However, one could not rule out that Esad would be back. His personal army roamed Central Albania and challenged Zog's and the government's authority. Sitting on the outskirts of Tirana, the soldiers waited for word from Paris to take Tirana, sell out the north to the Serbs and the south to the Greeks, and create an easy to manage feudal enclave in the center.

But there were people other than Zog who wanted a European Albania. Avni Rustemi saw an opening for countries like Albania to finally shake off the Ottoman legacy of landlords, Islam, and the likes of Esad Pasha. Everyone else had done it. What held the Albanians back was their conversion to Islam, which tainted them in the eyes of the West. Heroic images of Albanians shaking off Turkish rule eluded them. Albanians had been massacred just like the Greeks on Chios in 1822, but according to popular opinion, the Albanians simply had it coming for collaborating with the Turks. There was no Eugene Delacroix, who painted the Greeks as they were slaughtered on the island of Chios, to paint the fate of the Albanians for the salons of Paris. Until then, every Christian Balkan nation had leveraged religion for sympathy. The Albanians were always in the same basket as the Turks—just a little version of Turkey.

Even by the standards of the time, Rustemi was a real democrat, and he temporarily bought into Zog's veneer of a western Albania, culturally linked with Italy. In Tirana, Rustemi and Zog possibly plotted Esad's murder. By 1920, assassinations were mainstream in Europe, and not just Albania. There was Empress Elizabeth of Austria-Hungary in 1898, the king of Italy in 1900, the king and queen of Serbia in 1903, the prime minister of Spain in 1912, the Habsburg archduke in 1914, and the king of Greece in 1918, among others. Rustemi and Zog agreed that assassinations paved the way for a new political order. For Rustemi, Esad had to go; otherwise, he would sell the country out to the Serbs in Paris for the sake of a sack of cash. It is highly probable that Zog agreed that Pasha was their primary obstacle. Zog knew early on that a few well-timed assassinations could change everything.

Esad's betrayals were legion. By then, Rustemi and just about everyone else knew that Esad had handed over the Albanian town of Shkoder to the Montenegrins for cash, sending a note to the Great Powers explaining that he had left a "valise" there and that as long as it was returned, he would withdraw his troops. He then ordered the murder of his closest comrade, Riza Pasha, for opposing the plans. Assassinate Pasha and everything was possible. Rustemi decided to act.

Rustemi spoke perfect French. He would travel to Paris and take his chances. The French loved Esad for his service in the First World War; he was an officer in the French Legion of Honor, and he had the Croix de Guerre too. He was the man who could give Albania the stability everyone assumed it required. The old iron hand again. So flamboyant and greedy for the admiration of the crowd, he would be an easy target. Fat, living in a palatial apartment in the Bois de Bologne with a young Parisian girl, often drunk on rum and gambling like mad while dressed in his military garb, he looked the part of a Balkan warlord on holiday—just a cliché or a stereotype. Traveling from Rome, Rustemi left for Paris, telling no one of his plans. He arrived on June 4, 1920. Knowing he would end up in a French court, he bought a new suit and took a room on Rue du Faubourg in Montmartre for a month. In his tiny suitcase, he only had some extra underwear and some cash. The ever-austere Rustemi spent almost nothing.

He spent the next few days acquainting himself with the habits of Esad, who was extremely predictable—where he gambled, where he ate, where he drank, and where he lived. It was all very easy. It was the twilight of the Paris Peace Conference and Paris was still awash with people from the major and minor states. Treaties had been signed with Germany, Austria, Bulgaria, and Hungary. Europe had been remade with new maps—those of the winners and the losers—and the world seemed on the brink of something new and beautiful. Parliamentary democracy and national self-determination had triumphed. No one expected the low-level civil wars and world wars that followed.

Albania ended up as neither winner nor loser yet again. It barely survived as a tiny state and was handed over in ironic fashion to Italy for safekeeping—something that would come in handy when Mussolini would later look to justify an invasion. Austria was out of the picture Vienna could no longer help them. The American president, Woodrow Wilson, stepped up this time to save Albania from its rapacious neighbors, but future survival still entailed the removal of the country's foremost opportunist: Esad Pasha. He was due to return to Tirana in a matter of days to start making trouble and his private army was ready. Rustemi's dreams of a western republic free of its Ottoman past would be shattered, and Zog would spend his days as a pathetic number two or even three in his uncle's hierarchy of one. No Western bride, no tourist-filled crypt for sure, and no tiny kingdom.

Things went Rustemi's way in front of Paris's Hotel Continental, just across from the Tuileries Gardens. On a packed Paris Street on the afternoon of Sunday, June 13, as Esad and his girlfriend were about to get into his car to head to the races at Longchamps for the Jockey Club Prize, Rustemi brazenly killed him. As planned, hundreds witnessed the crime. Esad died instantly with two shots to the chest. An 11-millimeter bullet went right through his heart. So successful was Pasha's ruse that the Paris papers proclaimed wrongly that the president of Albania had been assassinated. Rustemi was no Gavrilo Princip, who, after shooting the archduke in Sarajevo in June 1914, hoped to kill himself by swallowing cyanide that no longer worked. Rustemi simply surrendered and awaited the consequences. His job was done. Let the court decide. The normally hot-blooded but baby-faced Rustemi was totally calm as the crowds rushed to watch Esad bleed out on the street. Rustemi just sat on the curb and waited for the police to arrest him on that beautiful Sunday afternoon. He did not flee. He felt good. His conscience was totally clear, and Albania had a future. So did Zog. He had done the most patriotic thing possible. In some ways, Rustemi got lucky as by any estimate there were at least ten groups in Paris plotting Esad's murder.

Rustemi always insisted he acted alone and never implicated the government in Tirana or Zog, for that matter, which would have been dangerous in the subsequent trial. The French prosecution wanted the death penalty, but, in the end, Rustemi was acquitted and returned to Albania a national hero. The trial took some unusual turns over the course of the summer. In what was clearly a first, both the dead Esad and France ended up on trial, and Avni's legal team essentially proved that Esad was a traitor who deserved to die. The court brought in historians to pour over Esad's dark past. Yes, he saved the Serb Army during its retreat through Albania in 1915, but he sold the Albanian town of Shkoder in 1913. One witness called him a "professional assassin." Moreover, even French foreign policy in Albania came in for criticism as they had enabled him throughout. Esad's lawyers desperately tried to portray Esad as a Francophile, but the historians mostly disagreed. Esad was on the side of whoever paid him the most and held no strong opinions about much of anything. For politically aware Albanians, he was a traitor. France could prove its noble motives only by acquitting Rustemi and ultimately blaming France for its failures in Albania. It was merely a crime of passion. France, the country, performed a *mea culpa*. This was something entirely new and totally unexpected.

The verdict was a huge achievement, thanks partly to the outpouring of support from Albanians everywhere who rejoiced in Esad's death. Long before Zog forced them to do it about himself, the peasants of Albania sang songs about Rustemi, hailing him for saving Albania.

As Rustemi told the papers, "I acted voluntarily and feel no regret. I have killed for Albania." He told the Paris court that his act was like the storming of the Bastille in July 1789, which really resonated, although the judge chastised him for the comment. Esad was just another Louis XVI who stood against the unassailable nation, and an entire nation could be neither wrong nor guilty. The court believed him, and he avoided the guillotine. The judge concluded that Rustemi's—and by extension, Albania's—grievances justified murder; Esad was a traitor who simply deserved to die in a Paris Street. Rustemi paid a token fine and, as a local celebrity, returned to Tirana and joined Zog as a member of parliament. By then, at least in Tirana, Rustemi basked in his glory.

In something incredibly telling, after lying in a kind of state in Pasha's villa in Paris's 16th district, Pasha's corpse went unclaimed for fourteen months, as it was later left in a Paris mortuary for 1 franc 50 centimes a day. Nobody dared claim it, as nobody in his family wanted to bear the expense of getting him back to Albania and building a tomb for him. Nobody knew where his money was, either. In the mortuary, the once powerful warlord, decorated for his service in the First World War, was merely known as number 17. Left almost without mourners, Albania's greatest war-lord was finished. Thankfully, the Serbs came to his aid and he was buried in a Serbian military cemetery in Paris in 1921. The Serbs were always grate-ful for Esad's help in facilitating the Serbian Army's epic retreat through Al-bania in 1915 and 1916.

Rustemi's success in the Paris court emboldened others who saw a chance to justify murder for past misdeeds and launch a new type of inter-national justice. In March 1921, an Armenian named Soghomon Tehlirian assassinated former Ottoman Minister of the Interior Talaat Pasha in Ber-lin as a part of Operation Nemesis to take revenge for the Armenian geno-cide of 1915. Pleading guilty like Rustemi, he was also acquitted in June 1921 by the German courts for not being criminally responsible for his deed in a trial that lasted only two days. And again, in Paris in May 1926, the Jew-ish poet Scholem Schwarzbard assassinated Ukrainian nationalist leader Symon Vasylovych Petliura, who was known for organizing Ukrainian po-groms against Jews in which Schwarzbard's parents allegedly died in 1918. Despite Schwarzbard's guilty plea, in October 1927, after eight days of delib-eration, the French jury pronounced Schwarzbard not guilty, arguing that it was Petliura, not Schwarzbard, who was guilty of murder. Schwarzbard gained fame as a national Jewish hero. Rustemi would never know just how inspirational his Sunday in Paris would be when states decided they could, in a way, undo past wrongs by justifying murder.

Back in Albania, there were additional successes. In the summer of 1920, Zog helped oust Italian occupying troops from Albania and earned the lasting enmity of the rising star in Italian politics, Benito Mussolini, who swore to avenge Italian humiliation in the Albanian town of Vlora, which he called Italy's "Albanian disaster." Mussolini hated the very exis-tence of Albania, which was proof of Italy's failures in the First World War. With these successes, the drama of making a small state shifted elsewhere. Albania's representatives were at the opening session of the League of Na-tions in Geneva with two things in mind: ensure Albania survived as a state and find a new king. Wied's return was entirely out of the question, no mat-ter how much he pleaded for his old job back. A German king might have worked prior to 1914, but certainly not after starting a war that ruined everything, and plus, Wied had actually fought on the side of the Germans. Meanwhile, Albania's representative to the League was Fan Noli, a graduate of Harvard, a somewhat self-proclaimed priest, and a bishop in the Albanian Orthodox Church who looked the part. In 1919, he almost wept as he praised the League's vision in admitting Albania. Noli was later destined for brief greatness as Albania's prime minister for six months in 1924, and Zog's foremost opponent alongside Avni Rustemi.

In Geneva, Noli took it upon himself to choose the all-around perfect person to be Albania's new king. His choice was the Englishman C. B. Fry. Fry was good at many things: politics, cricket, rugby, love, tennis, and everything else. Plus, he knew it. He also happened to be in Geneva in 1920, but inside the Indian delegation with his old cricket buddy Ranjitsinhji, fighting the good fight for liberal internationalism. Albania needed someone rich and preferably British to become king. There was a strange fetishizing of all things English among decision-makers at that time. An English gentleman, with experience in colonial rule, would fit the bill. Wealth was a prerequisite so that they could cover their own costs and maybe help fund the new state. Fry was perfect, and he impressed Noli with his lavish hospitality, paid for by Fry's friends. Things looked good, but Noli lacked the authority, and Fry was unsure about the expense—could he afford to be king? The offer faded.

Aubrey Herbert, the intrepid Balkan traveler and inspiration for John Buchan's character Sandy Arbuthnot in the novel *Greenmantle*, was another contender. There were other links to Buchan—the protagonist in his *The Thirty-Nine Steps*, Richard Hannay, thought that Albania "was the sort of place that might keep a man from yawning." In any case, the very real Herbert was a tireless promoter of all things Albanian, the equivalent of what Byron was for the Greeks in the early nineteenth century, who later became one of the most ardent supporters of Albanian independence. Herbert was the preferred candidate of the Muslims owing to his laudable stand against the violence perpetrated against the Albanians during the Balkan Wars. Herbert was also the most vocal defender of Albania's right to renewed independence after the war. Finally, Wilhelm of Wied's only son, Carol Victor, was, to nobody's surprise, also available, as he was only seven years old and obviously unemployed. Nobody could know then that Albania would have to wait eight more years for a homegrown king.

Back in Tirana, Zog was opposed to another king. In fact, he was the biggest opponent of monarchy among all Albanian parliamentarians. It was likely then that Zog had decided that he was to be king. Zog was livid with Noli's interference and fulminated to his mother about him. Noli was added to his list of people to get even with. The new government in Tirana eventually decided to mimic Hungary and establish a regency to represent a king who did not exist. The question of monarchy or republic was shelved for the foreseeable future.

The murder of Esad did not easily turn Albania into Switzerland. Instead of embracing progressive ideas as pledged, Zog, as prime minister, became more like his dead uncle. He allied himself largely with Albania's large feudal landlords—the seven big families. Zog brought into his retinue his old friend, the pro-Serb Ceno Bey Kryeziu, who married Zog's sister, Nafije, in 1922. Zog was even engaged to the daughter of the country's largest landowner, Shefket Vërlaci, but that proved to be an altogether temporary and strategic move, which would later haunt Zog and enrage his would-be father-in-law. Not quite a blood feud offense but close. These moves clashed with Rustemi, whose hero status made him the spokesperson for a progressive and maybe even democratic Albania. He wanted the Albanians to be the twentieth-century version of the nineteenth-century Greeks, who blasted away the Ottoman system completely and anchored Greece to the West forever. The feudal lords hated him almost as much as the local diplomats, who feared his progressive ideas would Bolshevize Albania and end the lucrative system of clientelism and resource exploitation that provided so much easy money to the diplomatic corps. The threat of communism, more perceived than real, would shape Albanian policy between the wars.

Rustemi joined forces with the largely Orthodox Christian Albanians who had emigrated from Albania's south and settled primarily in the Boston area of the US. Their experiences in the United States made them natural enemies of Zog and the Muslim ruling class. Rustemi established a number of youth-based organizations that pushed for, among other things, the total liberation of Albania's peasants, which for Rustemi simply meant the end of Albania's feudal landowners by whatever means possible.

Emboldened by his success in Paris, Rustemi decided the best thing for Albania was to murder Zog. Since so many people were thinking the same thing, someone else tried before he could hatch his plan. In March 1924, a young student, Beqir Walter, shot Zog in the parliament. Zog came out of the whole thing looking relatively good—even as a hero. Covered in blood after being shot, he urged everyone in the parliament to be calm. To recover from his wounds, Zog resigned as prime minister. His reaction to the whole thing reinforced the notion that Zog was the very symbol of stability. But the killing did not stop.

Unfortunately for Rustemi (and the would-be assassin), the first assassination attempt on Zog failed. Once arrested, Zog's men tortured the poor soul, hanging him from his arms for 24 hours and nearly beating him to death until they got the answer they were looking for: he falsely confessed that Rustemi put him up to it. Even though he later recanted and said he acted on his own on a blood feud debt, Zog maximized the whole business for political purposes. Time was running short for Rustemi, who now hoped to abandon Albania altogether for a new life in the United States. He even had his visa.

Taking a page from Mussolini's playbook, Zog understood that to be the law-and-order person and the source of stability, you needed to create the very instability and fear so that you could offer yourself as savior. Long before coming to power, Mussolini and his black shirts had killed hundreds of people deemed political opponents. The tools of a tyrant are quite limited—a bomb placed in a crowded marketplace blamed on your opponents or random killings to instill fear.

Zog's next attempt to stir things up, however, went too far. On April 6, two US citizens were ambushed and shot dead near Kruje, just north of Tirana, while on their way to Shkoder. The reaction from the U.S. press and government was severe and the Albanian government was especially concerned about the implications of the murders. Foreigners traditionally enjoyed the protection of the *besa*. Almost impossible to translate into English, *besa* can mean truce, protection, or word of honor. In the case of the Americans, it was most certainly a pledge of honor exempting foreigners from harm that is explicit in the *Kanun*. As such, they should have been untouchable, but mistakes happen.

Besides this, the government could ill afford the adverse press which always portrayed Albania as a savage backwater rife with thieves, brigands, and murderers. Accusations of lawlessness played directly into the hands of Albania's neighbors who argued all along that the Albanians were not ready for self-government but preferred anarchy instead and here was the proof. Albanian brigandry was music to the ears of the politicians in Athens and Belgrade.

News of the shooting spread fast, and before long the international media had picked up on the notion that either current or former members of the government had been involved. The government did its best to head off a barrage of criticism. Nobody except Zog and the assassins knew just who was responsible for the crime. At the outset, US officials in Tirana seemed to think that the crime was political. Those in the know sensed that Zog had orchestrated the murders in the hope of convincing everyone that without him in power, things simply fell apart. The problem was that Zog hired poorly trained people who had never actually assassinated anyone before. He gave them notes as to what to do, but Zog forgot or did not know that the team was totally illiterate. The written specifics were lost on them. They only knew to wait by the road in Mamuras for two men traveling north in a car. Who could have expected there would have been two cars headed north that day in a country with fewer than 50 cars? They stopped the first car and shot the driver and passenger. The car that followed later that day was the intended target. The assassins would later be hanged in Tirana for their crimes. They tried to blame Zog, but their illiteracy got them again. Why would Zog give illiterate people written instructions? Zog was too smart for that, the court concluded.

Zog did not stop there. Allied with Fan Noli, Rustemi had become a major opponent and obstacle. Zog had to act, so he hired a former servant in his house, Isuf Reci, likely a hapless drunk, to kill Rustemi. On a quiet Sunday afternoon on April 20, Rustemi walked with two friends from the New Bazaar in central Tirana to the cemetery to pay respects to a dead relative. Rustemi and his friends had just crossed Tanner's Bridge, built as a footbridge by the Ottomans for traders to cross Tirana's Lana River to connect with Albania's north. Rustemi loathed the Turks, but he loved the architecture they left behind in mosques and bridges. Crossing the bridge, Reci sat in a nearby café of sorts—just a kiosk, really—with some straight-back wooden chairs to sit on outside near the cypress trees that stood by the bridge. Reci certainly had his usual local raki. It was too late for coffee, he maybe decided. Zog told him to stick to the rules of the *Kanun* and not shoot Rustemi in the back. He forgot that part—Rustemi was shot in the back, twice. But he was also armed and fired back four times but missed. Rustemi died two days later. Zog badly miscalculated, again. Everyone knew he ordered the killing and his opponents gathered strength. Rustemi was the martyr everyone was looking for. Reci, on the other hand, headed for Mati, where Zog protected him and gave him a job at the local prison. During the war, long after Zog had fled, the communists would execute him. Rustemi was one of the few heroes of the period the communists could embrace.

Rustemi's funeral on April 28 brought the biggest crowd that Tirana had ever seen; Zog had ultimately murdered the most popular politician in Albania. This was likely one of the few truly spontaneous moments in a country where public displays were invariably state-sponsored. His body was laid out in the center of the capital. Thousands came to pay homage before Rustemi's corpse was sent to Vlora on the coast for burial. For some strange reason, Avni's heart was preserved in a jar in a pharmacy in Vlora. Revolution came not long after as Zog's opponents, a mix of progressives, careerists, and opportunists, joined forces to run Zog out of the country. The new government had only one goal in common: Zog needed to be murdered. Zog did just what his uncle would have done: to avoid being hanged by the new government, he fled to Serbia, where the Serbs were just as happy as the Austrians had been in 1917 to have him in their hands in the hope of using him to further Serb goals in Albania. He left his mother, sisters, and nephew behind. The Zog epoch was over it seemed. A revolution had started. Or maybe it was just a coup. The difference was never clear. No one could really tell. Zog chose to bide his time in Belgrade and wait for the bidding to start and the unity of his opponents to falter.

Chapter Five

A Taste of Exile

Rustemi's murder turned the tide against Zog. Rustemi was popular, and his legacy in Albania would certainly outlive Zog's. In a century that was nearly bereft of untainted heroes, Rustemi would be remembered as someone who sat squarely on the right side of history. In June 1924, Zog was forced to flee Tirana as a ragtag band of soldiers, social revolutionaries, ideologues, opportunists, and Albanians from Kosovo unhappy with the borders took over Albania and tried to make it Western and European. They called it a revolution, but it was not. Like most revolutions, it started with violence and ended in total failure, partly because of its own shortcomings but also because external factors worked against its success. To start with, nobody actually believed the Albanians could make a democracy. More importantly, onlookers viewed the revolutionary goal of destroying Albania's feudal order as dangerous Bolshevism.

In what was to become a habit for any Albanian leader on the run, Zog emptied the Albanian treasury prior to abandoning ship and used the funds to stay afloat during what he hoped would be a short exile given that he had to leave five of his sisters and his mother behind. The choice of Belgrade was an odd one, especially given the savagery Zog had witnessed from Serb soldiers towards Albanians in the First Balkan War. However, pragmatism prevailed and choices were more or less made for him. The Serbs were hardly supporters of an independent Albania. On the surface, Italy would have been a better choice, but Mussolini loathed him and the Greeks held a similar opinion. Mussolini had been in power since 1922, after the king and Italian big business handed him power to stave off a civil war.

Mussolini's grand dreams of a new Roman Empire, or maybe the Venetian Empire, were known, and his desire to make Albania an Italian playground was obvious from the start. Moreover, the Italians had far more money than the Serbs. But Mussolini would have to wait for Zog to sell out to the highest bidder. If there was one thing Zog had learned from his uncle, it was that playing Italy against the Serbs could yield results. Given Ceno Bey's influence in Serbia, Zog's entourage was welcome in prime minister Nikola Pašić's Kingdom of Serbs, Croats, and Slovenes, and he found himself again in another Hotel Bristol, but this time in downtown Belgrade, not Vienna. Belgrade's elite was delighted with his choice, and Zog found himself once again as the exotic playboy in a foreign capital, feted by the local elite whose spies watched him hoping to create the most wonderful opportunities for future blackmail. The Serbs had Zog just where they wanted him, and Ceno Bey was always ready to take his place if it came to that.

In Tirana, the new government tried to make a western and democratic state on a field of ruins with no cash. According to his detractors, Noli's sonorous voice and bombastic phraseology worked on the illiterate and half-educated, which was 95 percent of the population. They set up courts and tried Zog and his minions in absentia for the litany of murders they committed. Zog and almost everyone else got a death sentence in what were spectacular show trials. The poor soul Zog had paid to assassinate some foreign diplomats, but who killed two American tourists instead, was hanged in what passed for downtown Tirana. In keeping with the *Kanun*, they left Zog's mother and sisters out of the trials. Only Nafije had left with Zog to Belgrade. The rest of the family returned to the castle in Burgajet.

Out of money, the new government appealed to the outside world for help enacting their plans, but none came. Everybody assumed a democracy in Albania was ridiculous. Keep your expectations low and be happy was the mantra of the Great Powers and the local foreign diplomatic corps. Everyone liked Zog—he brought stability and cash, and they wanted him back. Bide your time, the local diplomats decided, and Zog will be back to sell the country off at rock-bottom prices. Besides, oil had been discovered in Central Albania, and the Americans, the British, and the Italians were after it. Everyone thought Albania was just gushing with oil. Zog had given everyone assurances that he would split it between the three interests in exchange for kickbacks. Noli foolishly hoped that he could use the revenue to advance Albanian national interests, like building roads and schools.

The Tirana government had some clever people with the right ideas, some real notables. Fan Noli, who tried to entice C. B. Fry to the Albanian throne, was the prime minister, and he was joined by some of Zog's greatest enemies: Bajram Curri, Luigi Gurakuqi, and Hasan Prishtina. Zog had banished Curri and Prishtina to the mountainous regions of Albania's north after they had failed to topple one of his previous governments. The outside world assumed they were dangerous rebel leftists determined to change the borders, unite the Albanians in one space, and make the peasants free. The prevailing ethos of the period was anti-left, whatever it might entail—Bolshies were to be jailed, deported, or murdered. Noli hardly spoke the language of class warfare—that would come after the Second World War when the Communists brought a real revolution—but Noli did speak of peasant liberation despite failing to ask the peasants if they wanted liberating. Noli's government could not overcome their differences to survive long in power. They fell out over Kosovo: Curri and Prishtina wanted to forcibly liberate it from Serb rule, while Noli, ever the optimist, believed that a new era was in the making and that the League of Nations would defend persecuted minorities. Noli was therefore content to try to get the Serbs to simply stop murdering or expelling the Albanians with appeals to global humanity. He was doomed to fail as the Serb goal was a Kosovo that was free of Albanians.

To that end, he made some horrible mistakes that increased the likelihood of Zog's triumphant return. On the one hand, Zog was loaded with cash. He had just been bribed by British oil interests to hand over a lucrative oil concession which he combined with the entire Albanian treasury, which he loaded into cars and headed north. Noli, on the other hand, could not buy off the army or the local warlords to keep the peace in order to implement his reform agenda. Plus, peasants could not be liberated from Zog's feudalism without cash either. Noli thought his agenda was of interest to the rest of the world, so he left Albania in August 1924, cap in hand, to find the cash to support his plans. The often-sanctimonious Noli failed everywhere he went: Rome, Paris, and Geneva. His sermon-style lectures alienated his would-be benefactors. Noli foolishly thought that the world would care about the fate of Albania. After lauding the League's chivalry in 1920, he heaped scorn on it for failing Albania. Nobody cared.

Returning home empty-handed, Noli's government collapsed in chaos as the warlords clamored for cash that he did not have. To his regret, Noli also discovered that he did not actually like living in Albania. He was, after all, not even born there. His American experience had changed him, and the world of Balkan politics depressed him. He was a bishop of the Albanian Orthodox Church after all—better to save souls than people. He likely concluded that politics was not his vocation.

If the international order in Europe worked against Noli, it certainly worked for Zog, who very much fit the low expectations set for Albania. Although the Belgrade in which Zog arrived was not the Constantinople of 1908 or the Vienna of 1917, it was a capital that was hardly like the Tirana he had just left. It had hotels, streetcars, electric lights, and prostitutes. Tirana was still waiting for its first Italian-built hotel to come in the 1930s. But Zog was not happy there as the Serbs viewed him with deep suspicion as his credentials were suspect. Hadn't Zog fought on the wrong side of the First World War? Hadn't he been an Austrian guest in 1917? The Austrian stink, as they called it, was hard to shake. The Serbs always looked for a new Esad Pasha, and suspicion surely lingered over the fate of Zog's uncle in Paris. Rumors abounded.

But he had his brother-in-law, Ceno Bey, who was adored by the Serb government primarily for his service to them in Kosovo, to hold his hand and make all the right introductions. When the Serbs occupied Kosovo in 1913 and again after the First World War, the Serbs could rely on him to bring stability through violence among the Albanians. Ceno Bey opened the doors for Zog to the Serb politicians and procured him prostitutes. Ceno Bey spoke Serbian, Zog did not. What were they talking about? Zog must have fretted. In Belgrade, Zog had to depend on him and for this, Zog likely never forgave him. Ceno Bey was ultimately a capable number two, a man who had married for political reasons. He was now taking on airs and distrust emerged.

Zog tried to make the best of his local celebrity status, but by the fall of 1924 his political capital was diminished. However, he still had all the cash the British oil men had given him. The Serbs expected him to go home and deliver on his promises. His garish military outfits stood out in the streets of Belgrade and he was the talk of the town, but he was fast becoming a joke. He gave countless interviews to the papers. Capitalizing on the hysterical anti-communism of the period, he successfully made Noli out to be a fanatical communist. Noli was the "Red Bishop" determined to communize Albania. That epithet, in that part of the world in the aftermath of the First World War, when Bolshevism was the principal bogeyman of the era, did Noli in. He was never able to shake it.

Maybe Zog's mother wrote to him to tell him of their plight and downfall, stuck in a shabby castle with a hectoring priest in power. If so, his mother was right. Zog had the cash to raise a small army, but if he was to make a triumphant return to send Noli packing, he needed more soldiers too. As luck would have it, the Serbs were happy to help him return to power for a number of reasons. For one, Zog was easy to buy, and he pledged to walk away from the Albanians who lived in Kosovo. Their fate, which was miserable, was not his concern, and they never liked him anyway. He promised to have their leaders murdered. Moreover, he bartered away some pieces of Albanian territory—some pastureland in the north and a gorgeous ninth-century monastery, Saint Naoum, on Lake Ohrid. As Muslims, the Albanian claim to a medieval Orthodox monastery seemed tenuous anyway.

In addition to his own 5000-plus tribesmen who were busy fomenting trouble on the border between Serbia and Albania largely by stealing sheep from the Serb side of the border so that the Serbs could later complain to the League of Nations about Albanian brigandage and border violations, the Serbs offered a thousand of their own soldiers plus over 20 million dinars in cash. But it still was not enough. Luckily, the Serbs had another army on their soil—the remnants of the White Russian army that the Bolsheviks defeated had decamped to Belgrade where they had converted themselves into a respectable mercenary army waiting for a war.

This White Russian army, under the leadership of General Piotr Wrangel, having lost to the Bolsheviks in the Russian Civil War by 1922, found themselves scattered in Bulgaria and Serbia. They were among the hundreds of thousands who fled the Bolshevik takeover. Wrangel and his men entered Serbia as honored guests with diplomatic privileges. The Serb king desperately needed an army, having lost his own almost entirely in the First World War. The White Russian army needed a country and for a time it was Serbia. In Serbia, some 150,000 soldiers and their families found a temporary home as they awaited the collapse of Bolshevism. They had also settled in Bulgaria and considered Hungary as well, but were turned down by the Hungarian regent, Miklós Horthy, because he had such a low assessment of the fighting skills of any Russian army... Red or White. Wrangel desperately sought to keep his army intact to be ready to invade Russia when the time was right. Lenin's Bolsheviks simply had to falter. But in January 1924, Lenin was dead and they were still stuck in the Balkans.

For Wrangel, keeping morale high and his army together proved difficult as most ended up in manual labor building railroads. They soon found themselves bored, drunk, underused, and dreaming of becoming taxi drivers in Paris. One of the army's key leaders sold rotten Hungarian cheese, hoping to pass it off as French Roquefort, as it really smelled bad. Others painted everything from houses to lampshades. A few thousand bored men who hated communists were a godsend to Zog.

Alongside Ceno Bey, Zog likely prowled the Belgrade bars with the mid-level White Russian leadership and cut a deal for 2,000 Russians to join them for an invasion. The catch was, in order to avoid having it look like a foreign invasion and invite international scrutiny, the tactician Zog decided everyone had to dress in Albanian national costume. The Russians never figured out who Zog really was; they assumed he was the king and referred to him as such. They never asked tough questions. Textiles and tailors were found, and the process began as the clock was ticking—Noli was back from Geneva and was planning to legitimize his government with an election. Zog had to get there before then. Legitimacy was the enemy of any decent Balkan potentate and Zog could never win an election. The impetuous Noli unwittingly made Zog's recruitment efforts easier when he broke the Golden Rule of small states after the First World War—he started talks with the Bolsheviks in the hope of playing them off against the Western powers. That news spread easily throughout the Balkans. A red Albania—where would that lead?

Sitting in Belgrade cafés, reflecting on how badly things had turned out in a never-ending exile, Wrangel's idle soldiers heard a rumor that an Albanian prince was paying money to overthrow a communist priest in cahoots with the Bolsheviks. It was a dream come true. Exile was costly, and two years out of Russia was a long time. Word spread quickly and before long, hundreds of exiled White Russians were amassing at the Serbian-Albanian border, getting fitted for Albanian costumes and handed guns provided by the Serbs. Wrangel was furious; he had banned his soldiers from accepting foreign military ranks, but they did so anyway. Wrangel already had the afterlife at the top of his mind: he concentrated on building the Belgrade Russian Church with a cemetery where he and his men could be buried according to their values.

Time was running short for Noli. On his way home from lecturing statesmen in Geneva, Noli stopped off in Rome in early December for a visit to the Soviet representative to Italy, Konstantin Yurenev (who would later be executed in one of Stalin's purges as spy...but nobody knew that then). Yurenev received Noli in grand style, with tea and crumpets, and Noli lapped it up. Finally, after indifference everywhere else, he finally got a proper hearing. Yurenev painted Noli perfectly, praising his speeches, quoting verbatim Noli's stinging critique of the League of Nations, and seeing him as a fellow traveler seeking social justice for the masses. Plus, the Soviets had cash to spare to help Albania.

Noli got caught up in the moment, and, with absolutely nothing to lose, he invited a Soviet delegation to open shop in Tirana. "Why not?" he probably thought, "what is there to lose?". Albania was about to recognize the Bolshevik government, which he thought was fine given most other European countries had done the same. But untrustworthy and weak states needed to play by different rules. This was an act of total desperation for Noli. Back in Tirana, he was attacked on all sides; Albania's neighbors were equally livid. When he realized the error of his ways, he tried to undo the damage with a telegram begging the Soviet delegation to postpone the arrival of the mission and wait until after the election. But the visas were issued and the tickets booked. The Soviets simply ignored Noli's pleas, and a Soviet delegation led by Arkady Krakovetsky and his wife set off by boat from Bari. They knew they were no longer welcome, but who could turn down the chance to create an international incident? They arrived in Durres and later Tirana on December 16—too late to be diplomats but perfect timing for Noli's undoing. Zog and his White Russians were about to start marching down from the mountains.

Indeed, on December 17, 1924, Zog, the White Russians, and the Serbs invaded Albania, and nobody outside of Albania said anything. At the border, the guards immediately changed sides, embraced Zog, and started shouting pro-Zog slogans. It turned out they had not been paid in months. Zog handed out some of the gold coins he had looted from Tirana in June. The Russians told the locals he was their king, and they rejoiced and shouted, "Long live the king!" Zog liked the sound of that. Zog's army marched on to Tirana, stopping in every town along the way for the peasants, who had been chased from their homes to a forlorn and dusty town square, to fete his return. It was a tough journey to Tirana as the roads were horrible, but it was hardest for the Russians, who were stuck pushing the heavy guns. The chance to kill some Reds kept them going. The Albanians were largely nonplussed; a new government for them was an ordinary occurrence. Everybody knew it was a foreign army—Russians don't look like Albanians, but nobody said a word. The Russians noted almost no resistance as they bore down on the "Reds." In the northern town of Peshkopia, the locals had shown the pragmatism that was a hallmark of their survival by setting up gallows. The Russians broke down the gates of Peshkopia's prison to free those jailed by Noli and everyone else. In Mat, the Russians joined forces with Zog's jubilant tribesmen. They encountered no resistance as they marched to Tirana. The tiny Albanian army surrendered and denounced the "Red Priest," who had misled them. Zog distributed cash. Life returned to normal.

As word spread that Zog was on the outskirts, the citizens of Tirana came out in the streets in jubilation, just as they had done when Noli came only six months before. They had grown used to being offered some incentives to spontaneously demonstrate fealty to the latest ruler, and the return of Zog a mere six months after he left was no exception. The business owners lied low, wondering when Zog's racketeers would be dropping by to help cover the costs of his return. An optimistic Noli had set up gallows too—one to hang the Russians and one to hang Zog's Albanians. But Noli knew then that if he stayed he would be hanged, so he prepared a hasty getaway.

The Russians came to loot and whore, but Tirana disappointed them, especially since there were no whores, no bars, and the town had already been looted so many times before that most of them headed back to Belgrade almost immediately with the small sacks of gold coins Zog had given them. But those that stayed looted the remaining stores and used the stolen products to open their own stores or set up checkpoints on the road in and out of Tirana to shake the locals down for arbitrary tolls. But before then, the Russians were greeted with a military orchestra in a town littered with flags. The Russians went to Zog's house to cheer their leader, but Zog did not come out to greet them. He was far too embarrassed. Instead, he sent Ceno Bey to distribute more gold and raki. The Russians were billeted in a large house with corridors that later filled with empty vodka bottles. There were a few receptions where the White Russians were given strict orders on etiquette. There was a ball with the Albanian officers and their wives, who were not permitted to wear veils and were explicitly told to wear French-cut dresses. The Russians were told to dance the tango and the foxtrot with them. They needed reminding not to crowd the buffet table and to eat with forks, lest they dirty the women's dresses or backs with their greasy fingers. A few others hung around Tirana as Zog used them to guard the parliament, and he sent a few to the north to disarm certain parts of the population and shoot anyone resisting. Some were offered citizenship and careers for helping Zog get rid of his enemies. As many as 15 hung around until Zog was ousted in 1939. As the Russians saw it, they had saved Albania from Bolshevism. Albania was not Russia, but at least they had one success in lives otherwise dominated by tragedy. Most certainly, they hoped to meet up with the Soviet delegation to hang them, but they missed that opportunity.

The foreign diplomats, knowing they had to choose between Zog's gangster mafia-style leadership or Fan Noli's irredentists and social revolutionaries, understood that it was always better to choose Zog's mafia as it was so utterly predictable. In the prime minister's office, sitting at the same desk that Zog had sat at and the same one Zog would occupy again, Noli's personal secretary arrived to tell him the Russians had taken Tirana and were smashing up the shops looking for booze. Noli had a weird soft spot for Russians, as he had been ordained by a renegade Russian Orthodox priest in the US, but this was too much. But he was conflicted, as the Red Russians were in Tirana too. Red and White Russians in tiny Tirana—did the Russians really have to ruin everything? In any case, his revolution disintegrated. It turned out the peasants did not want social justice but merely to be left alone. Looking out the window and down to the boulevard, Noli would have seen placards welcoming the Russians, in Russian. Some local peasants were setting up another gallows. Another group was assembling a tiny triumphal arch for the invading troops to pass under with the slogan "Peace to all." Enough was enough. Time was short. Revenge was in the air again, just like always. Noli started packing.

A British diplomat remarked ironically that he saw Noli loading a car with whatever was in the treasury, rumored to be only 25,000 pounds. If true, it was at least the eighth time the treasury had been emptied since Albania appeared again as an independent state in 1920. Noli and Luigi Gurakuqi, after claiming they would fight to the last man, drove themselves to Durres for a boat for Brindisi, Italy. Boarding the ship, Noli and Gurakuqi possibly caught sight of Krakovetsky and the rest of the Soviet delegation in total hysterics. Krakovetsky had tried to leave the hotel without paying, but the owner got it out of them as cash was not a problem. They had brought loads of Italian lire to buy off the locals and create a communist party from scratch. An Albanian communist party would have to wait a bit longer but, as it happened, time was on their side. On the ship, the outcasts never spoke, separated as they were by class on the boat—the Soviets were in first class, while Noli and Gurakuqi hunkered down below deck. There was no next move to plot. Much to Zog's pleasure, Noli took with him most of Albania's intellectual elite. Emigration, Zog hoped, would save him from an annoying opposition.

Noli never returned to Albania, but he later found peace in his own church in Boston. He wandered around Europe for a bit, trying to rally all the Balkan peasants to seek liberation from the likes of Zog and the rest

Zog as president, 1925.
Source: AQSH (Central State Archive), Photo collection of Ahmet Zog, no. 23973.

of the Balkan leaders. If Zog became the *bête noire* of the communists, who would later seize power in 1944, Noli was their unlikely hero. It was a role he rejected. Gurakuqi hid out in Bari for a time, relying on the generosity of the Albanians living there and Mussolini's unwillingness to hand him over to Zog to be hanged. But safety was short-lived. Curri and Prishtina headed back to the Accursed Mountains between Kosovo and Albania. For Zog, his obsession was to see them all dead, although the British ambassador ironically claimed that Zog was not vindictive and that had they remained, they would have been "free from molestation." That was a lie.

On Christmas Day 1924, Zog was back in power, and it was his turn to exact revenge on his enemies who had forced him into exile in Belgrade. Only Noli was lucky enough to come out alive and die as natural a death as possible in retirement in Florida in March 1965; he was one of only a few of Zog's opponents that remained "unmolested." That night, maybe Zog held a party for the foreign diplomatic corps who mattered: the Americans, the British, the French, and the Italians. He was especially grateful to the British and Italians who financed his return in order to ensure Albania's oil riches. Surprisingly, the Serbs were not invited. Zog had already cut his deal with the Serbs in Belgrade, and he was now moving on to bigger money.

Chapter Six

Blood Calls for Blood

By the time Zog fled Albania in 1939, at least according to the papers, he had incurred 600 blood feuds. In his office, one could wonder if he employed a person who maintained *The Blood Book*, which illustrated, like a family tree, the multiple ties to families seeking his death. It was an ugly list, based on ordered assassinations, false prison sentences, and rigged court verdicts, plus maybe the fathers of women he had spurned. Prone to sullenness, did Zog review the book periodically to stay on top of things? The growing number of people in blood debt forced him into ever-increasing isolation among a smaller and smaller number of people with limited skills. To gain some peace, he invited the northern tribal leaders to Tirana where, for cash and other incentives, they pledged their *besa* to his government and headed back to the mountains, determined to ignore Zog's government. With the Russians, he continued the disarmament campaign of some people but not others, and the Russians were hardly discerning in who they decided to shake down for weapons. Leaving the country became an even greater challenge for ordinary Albanians. Safety in Tirana was not a given. Zog ensured his security by clearing the town's trees of branches lest they hide a sniper, but outside the capital his opponents could control the field.

Zog took solace that Mussolini hardly left Italy either. His first time was in 1938, showing up in Munich as a normal statesman, after 16 years in power. So isolated was Zog that he could hardly enjoy the makeover of Tirana. He had to make do with looking out the window from his office.

Only eight years old when Serbia's King Alexander and Queen Draga were shot then mutilated with swords and axes by their own soldiers, Zog learned early on about the dangers of being an unwelcome king in the Balkans.

Never one to keep his word, Zog did keep his word to the Serbs in Belgrade. There was no way around that. Territory was handed over, and the Albanian-led rebellion against Serb oppression in Kosovo petered out for several reasons. But after those deals were closed, Zog's greed got the better of him as he shifted from dependence on the Serbs to the Italians. The payout was potentially bigger, and he started his loving embrace of Mussolini, who certainly did not return the love. More importantly, the glamorous Count Galeazzo Ciano became Zog's new hero, and Ciano played the part of a dutiful and loyal friend.

Marrying Mussolini's daughter, Edda, in 1930, Ciano went from journalist to diplomat to propaganda minister to Italy's foreign minister in 1936. He remained Mussolini's number one stooge all along the way. Alongside his wealthy father, Ciano had been with Mussolini since the beginning and never tired of fawning over his boss. Mussolini would later hand the Albania "file" to him, and it was in Albania that Ciano sought to prove himself to his father-in-law. An elegant and smooth playboy, Ciano, like Zog, was a professional liar in a time when there was no truth to be found anywhere. He was treacherous and without principle. Despite being married, he had countless lovers, always preferring much older women. Theirs was an open marriage. "Keep your heart a desert" was one of the great *bon mots* from Mussolini's thoughts on love.

In 1925, Zog was in consolidation mode. He appointed Ceno·Bey as minister of the interior, whose sole responsibility was the violent murder of the 1924 revolutionaries and the troublesome would-be Kosovo liberators. Zog assumed dictatorial powers and turned to Mussolini for help in their implementation. The establishment of a presidential republic meant that Zog had effectively ended the monarchy of Wied, who was still around, hoping for a second chance. That left Wied, but not his wife, who hardly relished a return to Albania, extremely unhappy.

Mussolini absolutely abhorred Zog, considering him nothing more than a low-level gangster. For Mussolini, the Albanians were primitive bar-

barians who betrayed the goodwill of the Italians. Zog was betrayer number one. He did not forgive Zog for serving with the Habsburgs in the First World War, and he certainly never forgave him or the Albanians for chucking the Italian army out of Vlora in 1920. For Mussolini, Zog represented Italy's failure during the First World War. After all, Italy won the war but lost the peace. Had they won the peace, Albania would be Italian, and Mussolini was determined to make that happen. But the invasion had to wait. If US President Woodrow Wilson had tried to make the world safe for democracy, Mussolini had to first make Albania safe for Italian business and vacationers. After all, the wealthy industrialists, who had so willingly heaped cash on Mussolini's fascist movement, needed to be paid back, and they would get Albania as their new gateway to the Balkans and the Middle East. The Serbs, he learned, were more than a bit upset about Zog's abrupt embrace of Italy.

But Mussolini had to bite his tongue. He wanted access to the oil resources and forests of Albania, which Zog delivered to the Italians and the British in early 1925. For his services, Mussolini sent Zog 5 million lire—almost a million dollars today. But Zog needed a favor in return. He needed someone murdered on Italian soil, and March 1925 proved to be a good month for murders. Mussolini must have given the nod.

Fan Noli was out of reach, but Curri, Gurakuqi, and Prishtina were in the neighborhood. Zog set his sights first on Gurakuqi, another darling of the Albanian national renaissance, who was a politician, polyglot, intellectual, poet, educator, economist, and linguist whom Zog resented for being all those things. Gurakuqi had remained in the Italian port city of Bari, the capital of the Italian region of Apulia. Mussolini's Fascist secret police had registered all the Albanians, and they knew exactly where everyone was. The new and old diaspora of Albanians there kept Gurakuqi happy and well-fed. Zog had begged Mussolini to repatriate the Albanian emigres who fled in December 1924, but Mussolini would have none of it. He said he would only help if Zog made further concessions to Italian interests. Mussolini even chastised Zog in a letter by telling him he would hold on to the emigres in order to overthrow him—if it became necessary.

But with the new oil deal, Zog politely asked Mussolini, through the Italian ambassador in Albania, if he would mind if he organized a murder on Italian soil. As there was never a shortage of people in Albania willing to perform bad deeds for extremely small amounts of money, he sent one of his retainers to become consul in Bari, who then searched for just the right person to do the killing. He needed someone to infiltrate the émigré community and work from the inside. He found the most pathetic person he could to elicit the sympathies of the likes of a cosmopolitan like Gurakuqi.

In Bari, Gurakuqi was happy. Educated in Calabria, he spoke perfect Italian, and he was known in the city. He was handsome too. He loved the Italy of the Renaissance but abhorred the Italy of Mussolini. He was always cautious, though, as he understood that Zog would try to kill him. Everyone told him to flee to the United States. At around 9 pm on March 2, Gurakuqi left the Hotel Cavour after dinner with friends. He walked its cobblestone streets, likely hoping someday that Albania could have its own bustling port city. Turning down Corso Cavour, he likely could have felt the winds shift. Gunshots rang out, and pigeons scattered from the roadside. Everyone started screaming. He was shot three times by Baltjin Stambolla, his very own cousin, who had been put up to it by Zog, Ceno Bey, and the ever-present dirty deeds specialist, the Albanian consul in Bari, Chatin Sarachi. The latter was, by all accounts, a cunning rascal who earned Zog's undying love before he wanted him murdered. Eyewitnesses later recounted that there had been one or two "lookouts" in front of the Hotel Cavour and identified Sarachi as one of them.

Mussolini pretended to be furious that Zog would order a murder on Italian territory. In fact, the police had been told to look the other way. Instead, it was enthusiastic bystanders that grabbed Stambolla, who clearly had expected not just an easy exit but a blind eye to further murders. The nearly illiterate Stambolla later wrote a letter to Zog and Ceno Bey begging for help. He asked for more cash and immediate repatriation to Albania. In a weird way, Gurakuqi would at least beat Zog back to Albania—in 1957, the communists brought his remains home from Italy, made his house in Shkoder a museum, and named a street after him. Zog be damned.

Gurakuqi's assassination was part of a much wider attempt by Zog, with Sarachi's help, to eliminate all the members of the Fan Noli cabinet who found themselves in Apulia with Mussolini's acquiescence. Zog sent at least one other assassin, who arrived in Bari by boat and headed to Brindisi to murder two other members of Noli's cabinet there. He was arrested while stalking a hotel where the two were staying.

Zog likely received the news of Gurakuqi's death with undisguised glee, remarking to a group of foreign visitors in Tirana that he had one less person to fear. In the evening, maybe he toasted his success with his brother-in-law? He did not admit doing it, but his remarks suggested that he felt Gurakuqi deserved it for his opposition to his government and his constant slagging of him. Gurakuqi, by then, was hardly a threat. He had little more than the torn clothes on his back and 350 Italian lire in his pocket. When Stambolla ended up on trial, the Italian government panicked. The Rustemi trial in 1920 had set a precedent, and Mussolini did not want Zog's government, as a key ally of Italy, to be on trial as the French government had been in 1920. A political process, where the outcome could not be controlled, had to be avoided. But this was the Italy of Mussolini; the courts in his time gave whatever verdict was required, and Mussolini easily determined the outcome.

Stambolla was acquitted because he murdered someone who was dangerous. Moreover, the court heard that the corrupt and wealthy Gurakuqi, implying that he had robbed Albania, had refused to help the destitute "refugee" Stambolla when he asked for help. It was self-defense, the court heard, after Gurakuqi proceeded to beat Stambolla with his cane on the boulevard. He had no choice but to shoot him. It was a Rustemi-like outcome—only turned upside down. One of Albania's most prominent intellectuals was buried in Italy. Hasan Prishtina gave the eulogy. Gurakuqi did not have a cane.

Bajram Curri was next on the list. The 63-year-old warrior, lovingly called the "Old Man of the Mountains," was still hiding in the rugged mountains of northern Albania, living off the kindness of the villagers who protected him. He had been there since December. He had a few loyal men left, but his hopes of ousting Zog and freeing Kosovo were lost. Ratted out by some locals who were bought out by Ceno Bey, Curri died in a cave near Dragobia, one of the most beautiful spots in Albania. He was shot by his own men who wanted to save their own lives, as Ceno Bey's men had the place surrounded. The communists later named a town after him near where he died. Unlike Zog, he was the subject of epic poetry and songs long before he was murdered.

Even with Curri and Gurakuqi out of the way, Zog could still not relax. External enemies were one type of threat, and Noli was still out there too. But there were internal enemies as well, ones not sitting it out in the Burrel prison. Zog decided that it was his brother-in-law, Ceno Bey, who was his most dangerous opponent. Ceno Bey had shown a keen understanding of how to work with Zog. Since Belgrade's transgressions, he had again served as an able number two and a yes man. But he had started to take on airs. Ceno Bey knew about Zog's poor health, and there were whispers he was the heir apparent. He knew that Zog's tolerance for having people in the room smarter than him was zero. He knew when to lie low, but Zog had the dictator's capacity for self-doubt, and he decided Ceno Bey was no longer an asset. Ceno Bey knew the sordid details of Belgrade and the shady deals Zog had made there. Ceno Bey was also the architect of the assassinations of Gurakuiqi and Curri. Zog wondered if he did that for him or for the Serbs in Belgrade. He couldn't be sure. Ceno Bey's loyalty was in doubt.

To get things moving in the right direction, in 1926, Zog first sent Ceno Bey as Ambassador to Belgrade as the new Ambassador to the Kingdom of Serbs, Croats and Slovenes. He was joined there by his wife, Nafije, and son, Tati. Ceno was the perfect person to smooth things over with the Serbs who were angry with Zog's embrace of Mussolini. Besides, Ceno Bey's stature in Tirana was on the rise and he had to be sent out. He knew far too much and had been at the forefront of the murders of Curri and Gurakuqi. Plus, he looked a lot like Ahmed Zog. Ceno Bey understood that this was hardly a promotion, but he made the best of it. By the summer of 1927, Zog had determined that Ceno Bey had gotten far too cozy in Belgrade, so he was again 'promoted'—this time as the Albanian ambassador to Czechoslovakia. He arrived in early October.

A mountaineer in the Prague of 1925 was funny, but Ceno Bey as an ambassador was even funnier. Until then, he was entirely accustomed to the grey zones and shady deals in Belgrade or Tirana, not the formality and legality of Czechoslovakia. Ceno Bey came from a world of smuggling where winks and nods did the trick. The Prague he arrived in then could not have been more different from Tirana. The Old Town, Charles Bridge, the Castle, and Czech superiority did nothing for him. He presented his credentials to President Tomáš G. Masaryk. The Czechoslovak state, carved largely out of the ruins of the Habsburg Empire, had emerged as something different than the rest of the post-Paris Peace Conference states. This was the first Czechoslovak Republic and, by the standards of the period, was a center of enlightened humanism and morality. It had nothing in common with Zog's Albania. The Czechs and Slovaks, unlike the Albanians, had been big winners in the Paris Peace Treaties. Ceno Bey both admired and hated them. He was certainly the last person one could see as an ambassador to a state like Czechoslovakia. But in 1927, no one could have predicted that Albania and Czechoslovakia did, in fact, have something in common: both would disappear from the map of Europe.

Apparently, Ceno Bey always finished his day with a nightcap in the main square. Arriving in Prague's Café Passage on Wenceslas Square on October 14, he remained preoccupied by French art. He had probably barely sat down when he was shot multiple times by an Albanian student, Alqiviadh Bebi, who sat at a corner table waiting for him. Ceno Bey died on the spot. Like Rustemi, Bebi remained on the scene to be arrested. According to rumors back in Tirana, Zog wept non-stop for days upon learning about his brother-in-law's death, especially when foreigners were present. He vowed to put Ceno Bey in the family crypt that was still in the design stage.

At his trial in Prague, Bebi insisted he murdered Ceno for his betrayal of Zog. As luck would have it, during the trial, Bebi was shot and killed and died on the judge's table. His assassin, Zia Vushtria, was sent there by Zog to keep Bebi from talking. So, an assassin was sent after an assassin—and not for the first time. Ceno Bey, dressed in military regalia and lying in state, got a massive funeral—probably the biggest gathering in Tirana since Rustemi's funeral—and, in a surprising twist, a tomb which would elude Zog. Tati and Nafije were back in Tirana. Zog had another rival out of the way and his sister was a widow. The remnants of Ceno Bey's family fled to Yugoslavia to avoid further entanglements. Ceno's brother, Gani, would later turn on Zog and, further down the road, emerge and die as a key figure in the anti-communist resistance.

In 1928, Zog would be 33 and that meant a chance for one more big change—he would become king. Zog broke off his engagement to the daughter of Shefqet Vërlaci, one of Albania's largest landowners and the man who succeeded Zog as prime minister in 1924. The disengagement, thankfully, was not a transgression according to the Kanun of Lekë Dukagjini. Men could easily pay a small fine and move on. This was not the case for a woman, who could not reject her man unless she opted to stay unmarried forever. Regardless, Vërlaci's daughter did get married, but Zog's somewhat strategic thinking on marriage soured relations with Vërlaci, who vowed to get even. Zog knew this, so he started plotting to have his one-time prospective father-in-law murdered. He failed on that one. The tables would turn later: in 1939, it was Vërlaci who was plotting Zog's murder with Mussolini's encouragement.

After gaining Mussolini's approval to make Albania a kingdom, Zog started to prepare a weary population for another big change. In 1927, he had laid some groundwork when his minions in the mock parliament bestowed upon him the title "Savior of the Nation" based on his success in defeating the "Red Bishop." He was on the road to being King. "Spontaneous" demonstrations started happening to demand he take the crown. In a weird foreshadowing of more madness to come from the communists, his initials, AZ, started appearing on mountainsides. He really was bucking the trend in the aftermath of the First World War, where one republic after another appeared. But in the Balkans, monarchy persisted. He heard that Mussolini had a three-word slogan that was emblazoned everywhere: "Believe, Obey, Fight." He needed his own slogans.

His local spies started to spread rumors that he was related to Skanderbeg. Paintings fused his image with that of Skanderbeg. The development of an origin myth was critical to any good dictator. He started to write Albania's history to place himself center stage at key moments, setting the standard for his communist successors to later rewrite everything to remove him from history.

On September 1, 1928, Zog did his best to recreate the spirit of Mussolini's somewhat farcical 1922 March on Rome, when his tiny fascist party seized power through a violent insurrection and miraculously held on to it for twenty years. After all, Mussolini had taken a train from Milan to Rome after his fascist squads ran amok, destroying the printing presses of papers that might have been bold enough to print the truth. Beautifully choreographed, Mussolini knew the value of the staged entrance. He was appointed prime minister by a king who probably thought Mussolini was there to thrash him. By putting Mussolini in power, another social revolution was thwarted. Business leaders kept their cash and businesses. A weird status quo prevailed, however briefly.

Zog hoped to partially replicate the mass nature of Mussolini's moment, but there were no cities to occupy or ransack or opposition printing presses to destroy. Zog had no Black Shirts either. Moreover, Zog lacked a mass movement that could terrorize a population that simply wanted to be left alone. Like Mussolini, though, he argued that a change in the system would unify the people. It was intended to be a revolutionary change, a myth-making moment that would create the foundations of future legitimacy when generations looked back on what he hoped was a turning point. This might have worked in Rome, but certainly not in Tirana. Both countries did get foul dictatorships, nevertheless.

Thankfully, Zog's version was a lot less violent and there were fewer people involved. On September 1, 1928, there were no trains in Albania, so Zog merely went to the parliament to be proclaimed king. The locals were out too, wearing the usual embroidered vests and white pantaloons for the northern highlanders or the fustanella, the white pleated kilt typical of the southern Albanians. It was unanimous—all 200 deputies in parliament, eager to save their feudal property and their perks, were on side. Carefully choreographed, the parliamentarians, who had all been bought with cash and Zog's assurance that land reform was out of the question, offered him the throne that technically belonged to the exiled Wilhelm of Wied. If Mussolini had been put in power in 1922 by conservative interests eager to stave off revolution and civil war, Zog was the conservatives' choice too, as the status quo, especially feudalism, had to be preserved at all costs. The peasants got nothing in a system with non-existent voting rights and fraudulent elections. A similar scene would be repeated in Germany in January 1933, when conservatives and industrialists would choose a one-time corporal to run the country.

As a sop to the Albanians who were stuck living in always hostile neighboring states like Greece and Yugoslavia, a people whom Zog rarely thought about, he called himself *King of the Albanians*, not the more appropriate *King of Albania*. But that was taken from the French Revolution, when Louis XVI left behind his title as King of France to become King of the French, as the revolution demanded. The irony was not lost on those who knew that Zog had sold out or murdered the Kosovo leadership like Bajram Curri and hardly cared about the fate of the Albanians in the Yugoslav Kingdom. A tiny military parade followed and Zog's speech to the soldiers was hardly an oratorical achievement:

> I am particularly happy to note, to observe with my own eyes the solid steps the Albanian army has taken towards discipline and progress. Let us shout: Long live the army, long live the armed forces of the Albanian people.

No mention of God to be sure. After the speech, then came the muftis and the priests, Catholic and Orthodox, Tirana's emerging high society in fancy western dress, a whole lot of women in black veils, and the mountaineers in their white pantaloons and white fezzes. The sullen-looking sisters were there looking on in flappers and cloche hats. With excited school kids waving flags, Zog observed the whole thing carefully from a recessed position on a balcony, lest someone get a clear shot at him.

As ever, he had the tiniest mustache, wispy hair, a receding chin, and looked extremely anxious. Something about his face suggested that he knew the whole thing was a fraud. Tirana's garbage had been hidden behind the new Italian-built ministry buildings, and the city was awash in the symbol of the Skanderbeg flag—a black double-headed eagle on a red background. The new king declared a week of holidays. Shopkeepers all received the mandatory official portrait of Zog in military garb of course to display prominently, cap rakishly tilted. Italy was the first to recognize the new situation. Desperate for symbolism, Zog had hoped to don the crown of Skanderbeg too, but it was held in a museum in Austria, and the Austrians were intent on keeping it. He had one made of gold instead that weighed over seven pounds.

Leaving aside the Ottoman rulers who were out of work since not long after the end of the First World War, Europe got its first Muslim king and a new royal family. Possibly only Mussolini knew then that it would also end up being the shortest monarchy in recorded history—just over ten years. To justify the change, Zog always maintained that he was merely responding to the will of the people. (How he knew that was never made clear.) He would later claim that the monarchy was forced upon him by his people and the parliament. In an interview with a British newspaper, Zog acknowledged the shortcomings of his people but pledged to civilize them in short order.

For the next decade, Zog hardly left his home, spending his time chain smoking in his office, so afraid he was of assassination attempts. He told the Italian diplomat Pietro Quaroni that he was not against dying in battle but did not want to die in the street "like a dog." When he did go out, he took his mother or a sister or two with him, as a woman's presence acted as a shield from blood vengeance. Plus, despite his new title, no other head of state anywhere ever invited him on an official visit, and nobody, except Count Ciano, ever visited him. Ciano's dislike of Zog was deeply personal. Ciano was a noble and he could not accept that someone like Zog, totally without any pedigree, could become king. For Ciano, Zog was a "bandit" and a "so-called king."

Despite his feelings, Ciano was pragmatic and opportunistic enough to actively engage in thinking about Albania's future by trying to find Zog a wife in the Italian royal family. Early on, Zog had set his sights on Maria, daughter of Victor Emmanuel III, but that was ruled out in Rome. She was twenty years younger than Zog and she later married Prince Luigi of Bourbon-Parma, who had a far superior royal pedigree. His sister was Empress Zita, the last Empress of the Habsburg Empire. There were no other takers.

Zog did his best to make friends, but he was shunned even by other monarchs. He tried to look the part—he hired bodyguards, wore the nice suits, and bought a phonograph from the US to listen to American jazz. US newsreels told of his isolation as he listened to records alone in his office. Zog did leave Albania once. Hoping to make a splash, his trip to Vienna in 1931 for a tryst included a plea to the Austrians to return Skanderbeg's crown and a gun battle near the opera. That visit, as it played out, convinced him of the need to stay put. But he was in Vienna merely as a private citizen, hoping to find an intellectual and sexual soul mate à la Mussolini's lover Margherita Sarfatti (but less intrusive). Zog was not looking for political advice; all he wanted was to footsie with an Austrian heiress. Ironically, Zog would need to wait for exile to finally meet the other Balkan monarchs who were largely holed up in Egypt or the French Riviera.

Zog had made his claim to the throne as the guarantor of stability and the preserver of the natural order of things. Zog insisted that Albanians were in their hearts monarchists whose very ideals did not permit the understanding of a republic. He created a small royal court with an even smaller group of insiders, with his mother as gatekeeper and official food taster. A stern portrait of her hung in Zog's grand office. Zog perpetually worried about his authority; he was notoriously thin-skinned, so he was careful to avoid employing anyone educated to make him look like the smartest person in the room.

How to project authority, he must have wondered? Tackling illiteracy or malaria seemed a tall order and probably expensive. Vienna provided some inspiration, and monumental architecture seemed like a good idea. But that would not come cheap either. Street names were good too. He changed the new boulevard's name in Tirana to Zog the First Boulevard. He sent notes to the local prefects to name their town squares, if they had one, after him. He decided to build prisons for his enemies and to project a strong state. Prisons were cheap and would send the right message. Those opponents he could not kill, he would imprison. Albania was not the first country in Europe to abandon any trappings of democracy, but by 1928 it was just one more shabby dictatorship run by mediocrities eager to plunder the state.

He worked out a list of other easy fixes to solidify his rule: establish a royal mail like the United Kingdom, make stamps, issue new currency, and build statues. He began designs for the royal crypt in Burgajet. He would be entombed with his carved effigy on top holding a sword. There would be lots of photos of his past and a carefully laid out chronology of his life with lots of embellishments. A bronze statue would stand in the corner alongside a painting of his mother. Visitors would rub the handle of the sword for good luck. There would be a guest book too. He would be the first of a long line of Zogs to fill the hall, just like in Vienna's Capuchin Crypt. Like any good dictator, those who knew the truth were dead or exiled.

He decided to develop a national intelligence system too, one with international pretensions. Like most dictators, Zog received very poor-quality intelligence since the whole apparatus was staffed by his uneducated, sycophantic, and opportunistic tribesmen, who largely avoided giving him bad news. He balanced his foreign alliances. The British helped him build a police force, the Italians the army. He did set up a strong security agency though. Money was tight, so he offered small incentives to citizens who denounced their neighbors, friends, or family members for anti-Zog thinking. He also paid local snitches to ferret out opponents. It worked out almost too well, as before long, would-be informants lined up outside the new Italian-built Ministry of the Interior for the chance to create misery for a neighbor or loved one. In the Balkans, people took special pleasure in that. He also hired some retired British soldiers to help develop a national gendarmerie. He distrusted the army, as they had so easily abandoned him in 1924. But it was largely a phantom gendarmerie, where commanders invented names so they could collect their salaries and send some kickbacks further up the chain. He ordered a national disarmament but left his own tribe armed. He banned the blood feud, on paper at least.

But Zog was more concerned with his external enemies. Curri and Gurakuqi were gone, but there were others. He set about finding infiltrators for the remaining plotters from 1924, and they were mostly in Vienna, the bastion of émigré activity. He made a hit list: Fan Noli and Hasan Prishtina were at the top. Could he kill a bishop? The founder of the Albanian Orthodox Church? Of course, he could.

In the meantime, Zog wanted to work on another matter of external affairs: Albania's alliances. He was in deep with Italy since the Pact of Tirana of 1926 had made Albania all but an Italian protectorate that set Mussolini's benefactors up for riches in oil, forests, and tourism. Zog did not see the trap he was setting for himself; Mussolini had so much dirt on him, especially after Gurakuqi's assassination. His primitive understanding of international affairs meant he thought Italy had an interest in a strong Albania. Moreover, he thought Italy would help shake off its Eastern taint by linking Albania to Italian civilization. But the real model was much simpler: money flowed from Rome to Tirana, which Zog distributed to a network of cronies. Governing was the least of their concerns. When the pact was signed, the government brought the usual rent-a-crowd out onto Tirana's main boulevard to rejoice. For the time being, Mussolini likely concluded it was cheaper to pay Zog than to pay to occupy the country. Italy was not yet ready for military adventures.

Zog also hoped that Turkey's Atatürk would take notice of his reform agenda. But Atatürk deemed Zog an anachronism and Albania an "operetta." Zog nonetheless stayed the course in his ersatz westernization campaign. He bought his sisters a car so they could drive the Tirana-Durres road.

Chapter Seven

Making History

Three years into the new kingdom, and with some of his key enemies dead, Zog decided he needed a holiday. He also decided he could leave Albania. He left for three or maybe four reasons. He was in extremely poor health, largely because of chain smoking and allegedly exhaustion from over-work. He needed better care than was available in Albania. Nostalgia got the better of him, as he longed to relive his Vienna days. He also had two lovers there and he was still looking for a full-time wife. As for the king's health, nobody knew just what was wrong with him, but it was an open secret that he was involved with an Austrian dancer and her sister whom he had met in Novi Sad when he was in exile in Yugoslavia in 1924. The younger one, Franziska, or Franzi as she was called, was Zog's dream girl, but since they came as a package, Zog got stuck with the two of them, and that included the elder named Marie. After Zog's return to Albania, he brought Franzi to Tirana, where he kept her in seclusion as though she was in a harem. One Italian only got a glimpse of her but noted she was tall and had a shapely body. Zog knew eventually he would have to get married and not to her but, according to an Italian diplomat, he felt Franzi brought him good luck. In-deed, when Zog did finally marry someone else, his luck changed.

The Janko sisters, as they were known, had humble origins, daughters of a gardener, apparently, so Zog's kingdom bestowed the title of baroness on both. One was 25, the other 40, according to guesswork. Both women likely spied for multiple sides and reported back to whoever paid the most.

Zog loved anything Austrian, especially dirndls, and he also said an Austrian girl was the best combination of mountain hardiness and city polish. Zog lavished gifts on them from afar, courtesy of the state treasury. But he had to see them, so Zog and his entourage set out from Tirana by car to Durres, then by boat to Bari, then by train to Venice, then Trieste, then Vienna.

The Vienna trip brought Zog and his girls together again, albeit for the last time. Zog stashed the two of them in the nearby Hotel Regina, a Vienna landmark, across from the Votivkirche, just off the Ringstrasse. (Ironically, the Votivkirche has been commissioned by Emperor Franz Joseph's brother, archduke Maximillian, as thanks after the emperor survived an assassination attempt in 1853. The archduke would later become briefly the emperor of Mexico only to be executed.) Zog stayed at the more expensive Imperial right on Vienna's Ringstrasse. But when Zog was out and about, taking in the sights or drinking in the bars, he always had the two sisters at his side. Zog stayed for more than a month with no official business. The Albanian emigres living in Vienna, united in their loathing of Zog, had been told by the Austrian police to lie low or face immediate deportation.

So, Vienna offered world-class health care and some sexual servicing, with some culture thrown in. But there were risks to foreign travel. Back home, it was tradition for the locals to take advantage of the leader's absence to topple the government, so Zog took the necessary steps as he did not want to end up like Fan Noli, who had left Vienna for the United States just two months before Zog's arrival. Zog ordered the borders closed, but you could still bribe your way in or out. It was a random round-up designed to keep the peace while he was gone. The snitch office still worked wonders. They had to turn people away every day as the locals tried to advance their material interests with denunciations of neighbors and loved ones. On the train to Venice, one of his royal guards claimed he was robbed not once but twice by the same person. In Venice, unsurprisingly, the guard disappeared.

Even in the Vienna of the winter of 1931, Zog still succumbed to its charms, though the heady days of Klimt and others were a distant memory. It was a different city, as the fate of the new somewhat democratic Austrian republic was as uncertain as every other state in Europe. The low- and high-level civil wars between right and left that plagued Germany were replicated there too. Hard-core nationalists and copycat Nazis jostled with Socialists. An emerging form of Austrian-style fascism loomed. Vienna also held the remnants of many of Zog's opponents who fled in 1924—some 100 emigres there were always ready for a fight with Zog, and his visit was simply a provocation. Zog needed both medical help and girls. Plus, according to the papers, he had syphilis.

Zog had no interest in democracy or in Austrian politics. In between spa visits, bars, nights at the theater and opera, where he purchased adjoining boxes for the sisters, and steamy afternoons with them, Zog likely visited his favorite haunts from his first visit in 1917. Zog spent lavishly trying to get a reputation as a person with cash. He bought paintings and reportedly 400 silver egg cups, which he purposively overpaid for. He bought his girls fur coats—and some for his sisters back home too. He spent on the women so that they could look the part of real royalty. He ordered from a local jeweler a 2200-piece gold and silver service set inlaid with four kilograms of gold. As to art, his tastes varied, but he mostly preferred banal landscapes. Zog was hardly ever recognized anywhere he went, which possibly hurt his feelings. The local Mercedes company provided him with a posh car—a Mercedes Nuremburg model—in the hope he would buy a fleet for his government. On the night of February 20, his dream came true: he was finally front-page news in Europe. This was the second attempt to kill him; according to the local papers, the assassins had first tried to kill him in the park in front of the Hotel Regina.

On that evening, Zog likely sat idly chain smoking in his royal suite. He thought of nothing in particular but remained perplexed by the lack of official meetings. His dilemma was not unlike the one faced by his late brother-in-law in Prague—if anyone wanted to talk about Albania, they went to the Italian Embassy, where they could get results. But he took in culture. That evening, he was headed to the opera across the street but still demanded his chauffeur drive around the Ringstrasse for maximum visibility. Lots of confusion surrounds what happened to Zog that evening. Zog and the Janko sisters attended the opera *Pagliacci*, ironically about lovers and murders. Zog never liked opera, but he had to keep up appearances as a man of high culture eager to shake the mountaineer's veneer. He was simply doing what a king was expected to do. He would have preferred the Prater, the kitschy amusement park in Vienna's Leopoldstadt—a nice ride in a private gondola with dinner on the Wiesenrad, a few giggles and knowing looks in the hall of mirrors, and some cotton candy. His girlfriends liked opera even less, so fortunately they left early to wait for Zog at the nearby Winchester Bar. Zog and his entourage slipped out 15 minutes early, at precisely 10:15 pm. His many enemies, led by Hasan Prishtina, had every exit covered.

When Zog and his bodyguards exited, two assailants at two different exits, Ndok Gjeloshi and Aziz Cami, opened fire. Zog and the bodyguards fired back. Zog emptied his gun apparently. On the scene was also Chatin Sarachi, still one of Zog's men for dark deeds, who had been with Zog in Belgrade and who had helped facilitate the murder of Gurakuqi in Bari. Eager to always be the hero, in the subsequent trial, Sarachi later recounted the whole event as though he saved the king. Fact is, at least as the story goes, Sarachi fired so wildly that he nearly killed everyone. (Sarachi will appear later as an emissary of Zog's to offer haven for the Jews in 1939, still later in an attempt to blackmail Zog during his UK exile in the Second World War, and finally after the war as an impressionist painter of note living in London.) One of the attackers managed to jump into the café in the Hotel Bristol, right across from the opera, to tell Prishtina and his friends, who had been watching the whole thing from the café, that the mission was a disaster. They knew that already. Prishtina was livid. Cami and Gjeloshi were nabbed on the spot by an Austrian intelligence officer masquerading as a cigarette pedlar.

Zog was unharmed, but his main man, Major Llesh Topallaj, was tragically killed with two bullets in the head and three in his torso. Sadly for Topallaj, he looked a lot like Zog and this was intentional, as he was often called upon as Zog's body double. Another bodyguard, Eqrem Bey Libohova, was injured with a bullet to the leg. Some twenty shots in total were fired. Zog apparently shot five rounds. He cancelled the drinks meeting after the opera with the sisters at the Winchester Bar and fell into a deep depression but vowed revenge. He told the Austrian papers that he was certainly grateful no Austrians were harmed in the attack. Revenge was in the air again. The Austrian police concluded that Zog was much to blame for the incident, noting that everyone knew the Mercedes he borrowed and that he always insisted on having it parked ostentatiously outside whatever venue he happened to be in. On the plus side, the assassination attempt got him his first official meeting as the Austrian foreign minister showed up. German President Hindenburg sent a "get well soon" telegram.

Much of the Austrian press was off the rails in its condemnation of the Balkan abuse of Austrian hospitality in turning the streets in front of the opera into a vile gun battle—as though that kind of behavior was expected of Albanians. Austria's paper of record, lamenting that the country could not always protect itself against Balkan methods, said that the incident proved that the death penalty needed to be reintroduced. In the wake of the shooting, the Austrian police rounded up every single Albanian they could find. Those not charged were deported. Hasan Prishtina, one of the top opponents of Zog still alive, left Vienna immediately for Thessaloniki, Greece. In official statements, while Zog knew his own people were trying to murder him, he preferred to blame the Serb government in Belgrade in order to increase his importance to anyone willing to listen. The Serbs likely had so much dirt on him from his stint there in 1924 that he was more useful alive.

In Vienna, the two assassins, who screamed that Zog had "sold the country" and "long live freedom," were nearly torn apart by the local Austrian mob that descended on them in front of the Opera. The local media was careful to point out that of the two defendants, one was Muslim and one was Roman Catholic, so it was abundantly clear that religion had nothing to do with hating Zog. They were simply former Albanian army officers who were part of the political opposition to Zog. Arrested and put on trial in the fall of 1931, the two hoped to replicate the Rustemi moment—put Zog on trial as the king turned national traitor and kleptocrat who had sold out first to the Serbs, then to the Italians, enriched himself and his family, and left his people impoverished, illiterate, and deserving of death. They pointed out that the cost of Zog's month-long stint in Vienna was half a million francs and nearly bankrupted the country. Both men recounted the ruin that Zog had brought to Albania. Everything they said was true.

The attempted assassination and the death of Topallaj invited so much potential for more violence and blood feuds that the Austrians moved the trial outside of Vienna to the small town of Ried, some 200 kilometers west of Vienna. This was done not only to protect the accused from blood vengeance but also because rumor had it that the Austrians were worried about a trial in largely leftist Vienna would see a jury that would be happy someone tried to kill an oppressor like Zog and end up with an embarrassing acquittal just like Rustemi in Paris. The Austrian Justice Ministry wanted a guilty verdict. The defense desperately tried to convince the jury that one of the assassins was insane. Indeed, Gjeloshi sobbed throughout the trial as his lawyer spoke of a man destroyed by the very words "blood feud" since the age of three after his father was murdered. Tensions were so high that when a sport flier attempted to land in the town, the local authorities quickly assumed he was an Albanian there to bomb the town to smithereens. Although the defendants' stories later changed, the two claimed to have acted impulsively when the chance came. Cami said that on his way to a Vienna coffee house he met Gjeloshi, who told him he had seen Zog's car in front of the opera and he was off to kill him. Cami more or less said to his friend, "What a great idea! Let me go back to my apartment to get my gun." The shooting followed. When questioned by the judge as to what preparations had been made in the event they succeeded in killing Zog, Gjeloshi replied that plans were hardly necessary as the whole country was "longing to eat him up."

Back home in Albania, word spread incorrectly that the king had been killed in Vienna, which stirred panic in the landlords while the peasants and shopkeepers possibly danced in the streets. Zog's minions hastily prepared for an Albania without Zog. Who knows what went through their minds with news of the king's death. Given the natural order of things, it was likely decided that the crown should be offered to Victor Emmanuel III, the Italian king. But there was a glitch—the seven-year-old Tati was the real heir. This presented a conundrum, as they must have all agreed Tati was too young to be murdered. They would just kidnap him and stash him in the mountains. Everything was settled. But then news came that Zog was alive. The government promptly began another wave of arrests, especially after they received a telegram from Zog demanding that the government immediately devote themselves to organizing spontaneous celebrations of his miraculous survival. The dancing in the streets started again. The 1928 triumphal arch came out of storage, and everyone hoped that Zog never got wind of the plan to replace him.

Leaving Vienna, he abandoned the Janko sisters and never saw them again, although he continued to send them stipends as hush money until March 1939. The Austrian doctors told him to head to the Alps for the fresh air and more recovery. He demurred and went to Italy instead to make sure Mussolini did not get jealous after his lengthy stay in Austria. He stopped in Venice, but Mussolini declined to meet him. Who could know then that three years later, Mussolini would personally welcome a silly-looking and even nervous Hitler to Venice in June 1934? Hitler, in a weird trench coat and pointy shoes, looking like a salesman in cheap shoes, was decidedly upstaged by Mussolini, who at least looked the part of a dictator.

Zog made his way to the port of Bari to head by ship back to Albania. On the pier in Bari, he hardly gave a thought to Gurakuqi when the Albanian emigres turned up in enough numbers to denounce him. Fearing he was slipping deeper into despondency, to cheer him up his cabinet organized a massive welcome crowd when his ship docked in Durres. He raced to his Tirana palace where his mother probably prepared the usual meal, and he started to plot the next stage of his revenge. The trial in Ried concluded. Both men received relatively light sentences of two and a half and three and a half years. Zog's courts tried them in absentia in Tirana and the verdict was harsher: they received death sentences, had their property confiscated, and their families persecuted.

As for Fan Noli, he was more than disappointed that Zog survived. He entered the US for a second time in 1932 and was briefly interned on Ellis Island as a potentially dangerous radical. Zog's minister in Washington, Faik Konitza, under Zog's orders, intervened in Noli's immigration case to convince the Americans that Noli was a dangerous Bolshevik agent and unscrupulous agitator. In true Balkan fashion, Konitza, who counted himself as one of Noli's closest friends, had no issue denouncing Noli to the American authorities, although he did his best to cover his tracks. To their credit, the Americans had none of it and admitted Noli.

Between 1931 and his marriage in 1938, Zog got very jittery, and with good reason. Hitler came to power in January 1933 with some clear ideas about Europe's future. Thankfully, there were no Germans in Albania for Hitler to save and hardly any Jews either. His seizure of power, another bloodless revolution of sorts à la Mussolini, was, at least on the surface, the triumph of the status quo and the best guarantee that social revolution was delayed and private industry and property preserved. Big money prevailed. Zog thought Hitler's triumph was good news—military men in power. Hitler's attack on the post-war treaty structure did make Zog extremely nervous, but he felt comfortable enough that the Italians would always be prepared to support Albanian independence. He embraced the railing against the Bolsheviks, but Zog never got the business about the Jews. Zog did ponder where the Albanians would sit in Hitler's racial hierarchy. Still, he decided to leave the big decisions to Mussolini while Zog fiddled around the edges, selling forests and oil concessions for cash. Zog was hardly a strategic thinker. He did not play the long game but instead concentrated on wealth acquisition and staying in power. He put down a few rebellions in Vlora and Fier with loads of death sentences. Worried that Zog was going too far, the Italians intervened to commute them to life sentences. He grew increasingly isolated, particularly after his mother died in 1934. He could not even imagine recovering from that. He built a modest mausoleum in Tirana for her, with plans to expand it later based on his fanciful dreams derived from the Capuchin Crypt in Vienna. The communists could hardly wait to destroy it in the 1950s with bombs, grenades, and the scattering of bones. Did Zog ponder writing to Hitler? Surely Hitler's speeches irritated Zog. There is no evidence he asked for a translation of *Mein Kampf.*

It is unlikely that Zog could understand that Hitler's rants about blowing up the post-First World War order would end up costing Albania too. For Zog, the Albanians were descendants of the Illyrians which made them Aryans, according to his reasoning. Did Hitler know that? Zog's vision, such as it was, centered around preserving his power and his family's wider security, lifestyle, and perks. A return to an outhouse in the mountains was not in the cards. His state, such as it was, pledged the pillars of the French Revolution: Liberty, Egality, and Fraternity. Underneath were the pillars that governed much of the world then: a kleptocratic and parasitic state run by a small mafia of lofty moralizers making empty promises to illiterate peasants. Mussolini sent the big money to Zog, who took massive kickbacks for selling out Albania's resources. While the Italians got the better part of the oil concession, Zog kept his promise to the Americans and British and took hefty bribes from them too. The money just kept coming, and the family just got more and more brazen in their demands for more.

The inner court, the second tier of ministers below Zog's family, relied on the upward flow of cash from bribes for everything from a government job, especially one in the lucrative customs service or something cushy in a ministry, to a document to a scholarship for a child. Jobs for sale delivered cash. Remittances from Albanians living abroad kept many families from starvation.

Zog did try a few things to adapt to the spirit of the times. Hitler's attack on the Jews led Zog to become a champion of religious tolerance, with Albania's religions co-existing nicely. In his new role, if Zog could save the Jews, he could also save himself. This would prove to be one of three times Zog would attempt to use the Jews to stay in power. He decided, based largely on stereotypes, that he would invite some Jews to Albania to modernize it. At the time, there were likely only 200 Jews living in Albania who had largely settled in Albania in the fifteenth century after fleeing the Spanish Inquisition. Most ended up in what would become the Greek city of Thessaloniki. The Jewish resettlement plan was based on just another cash grab. Five hundred gold francs—a price nobody could pay—was the entry fee for any Jew that arrived. But border guards were easy to bribe and those that did come never paid the full amount. Still, Zog ordered his diplomatic corps in Europe to help get more Jews to Albania. To the immense credit of the Albanians, who had witnessed extraordinary sectarian violence from their neighbors in the First Balkan War, attacking a religious minority made no sense at all.

Herman Bernstein, the US ambassador to Albania between 1930 and 1933, helped Zog develop some pro-Jewish policies. Zog would even dictate to Bernstein a highly sanitized and truncated life story. Bernstein succeeded in making Albania a viable transit stop for Jews headed to the US, Palestine, South America, and Turkey. Zog's minions spread a rumor that Albert Einstein escaped via Albania with an Albanian passport. Zog needed good press. In 1934, Zog got serious about burnishing his image. He made a serious offer to grant Jews 10,000 hectares of partial swampland north of the port of Durres. The Jews were to live in an isolated colony of sorts of 5000 people. There was some momentum to the scheme—they had already planned for the machinery to drain the swamps. The plan collapsed as Zog's price was far too high. Zog got more cash from Mussolini instead.

To his credit, Zog was no antisemite, and neither were Albanians. He had no patience for the policies that Hitler was trying to force on his allies. It was Mussolini who forced him to adopt anti-Jewish laws in 1938, when Mussolini started to make life miserable for Italy's 40,000 Jews. Thankfully, Albania's majority Sunni Muslims had easily skipped the violence that shaped the end of the Ottoman Empire, largely against Christians, or the marginalization of Christians that marked Atatürk's new Turkey.

By the summer of 1933, Zog had to turn to more local problems. The once-Ottoman city of Salonika, the birthplace of Atatürk, was now the city of Thessaloniki. It consisted largely of Greeks and Jews, with no Muslims at all. But Zog's spies had informed him that Hasan Prishtina was there. The Greeks got the city in the First Balkan War in 1912 and set about making it as Greek as possible. A 1917 fire practically destroyed the place. Hasan Prishtina loved the old Salonika. Zog had met Prishtina in Constantinople during the Young Turk Revolution in 1908. Prishtina was even elected as a parliamentary deputy for Ottoman-controlled Kosovo, and he went on to become one of the key figures in the fight for Albanian rights in Serbia and later Yugoslavia. He was always fighting—against the Ottomans, then the Serbs, and finally Zog. By 1923, Zog had already put a hefty price on Prishtina's head. His role in Noli's revolution of 1924 only worsened things. He was also the key figure in the Vienna assassination attempt. Prishtina had to keep moving and had been on the run from 1926 to 1933. He often hid out in Vienna or Budapest. He was filthy rich, but no one knew how he made his money.

Zog replicated his success with previous assassinations. Working through trusted emissaries, he found a young fanatic to do the job. In this case, Ibrahim Celo, an illiterate fruit vendor and sometime resident of Barcelona, was hired to kill Prishtina. The plan had strange beginnings. Prishtina originally hired Celo to kill Zog. Celo and Prishtina first met in Nice, where he was tasked with Zog's murder. The details were sketchy. Prishtina promised Celo everything a peasant could wish for: a well-paying job in Greece, some gold, and a statue in Albania erected in his honor once Zog was dead. His mother could finally be proud of him. He would join the ranks of Rustemi in slaying a known and hated tyrant. He would become part of folklore. But Celo was cleverer than his total lack of schooling let on. He went to Tirana, made his way through layers of the royal court with urgent news for the king and told Zog his plans. Zog offered more money to kill Prishtina instead, but the statue was off. Only two people got statues in Zog's Albania: Zog and Skanderbeg.

Prishtina knew that Zog was after him. In his last will, he wrote that should he die "by a bullet from Zog...," he did not want to be buried in Albania until Zog was gone. In August 1933, Prishtina, a onetime prime minister of Albania and leader of the Kosovo insurrection, was shot five times as he walked side by side with Celo. He died on a street in Thessaloniki. Zog still could not relax. In 1934, the King of Yugoslavia and the French foreign minister were shot to death in Marseilles. He needed to get married and fast. An heir was required. Tati was not going to cut it. Zog needed to head west while remaining in Tirana.

Chapter Eight

A Royal Wedding

Zog's quest for a bride was something that consumed him for almost a decade after his breakup with Vërlaci's daughter. He had dozens of flings for certain, and there was Franzi, but he longed for a Western bride to burnish his veneer as a westernizer. The queen simply had to be foreign, as an Albanian was completely out of the question as it meant he would have to choose from one of the great landowning families, and that would mean upsetting all the others while also meaning that the spoils of the kingdom would need to be divided between two families.

Despite the obvious attractions of being Queen of Albania, there was a bit of a catch. The bride, quite simply, had to be rich and hopefully well-connected. So, throughout the 1930s, Zog fished around for a suitable bride who was rich and preferably from a country that might be able to help Albania, as the world was getting increasingly dangerous for small states. Zog pined for an American girl. The *New York Times* reported that he was "not bad looking." He took out several ads in US newspapers where he explicitly sought a US heiress. He told his diplomats in Paris, Vienna, Budapest, Rome, and Athens to send photos. His first goal was to get a princess from the Italian ruling House of Savoy with Ciano's help, but the Italian king thought Zog was merely a low-level gangster. He was then keen on getting a Habsburg, but he was later happy to learn that Greece was a monarchy again after a referendum in 1935, so he wondered about a woman from there. The Greek royal family showed no interest; Zog's lineage was suspect, according to their sources. The same was true in the United Kingdom, and he ruled out anything with the Ottomans, given his sister's fate. There was talk he would marry a woman from the Egyptian royal family. Nevertheless, Zog stuck to his quest for a westerner, plus the Egyptian dynasty, despite its Albanian origins, wanted nothing to do with the ersatz one in Tirana.

One such advertisement was explicit.

The King of Albania, Ahmet Zog the First, is seeking a wife from the United States of America who is also independently wealthy. While a level of beauty is helpful, the annual income required for the Queen is 1 million USD per year. The benefits of being Queen outweigh these costs. Interested women should send a photo and financial statement to the Albanian Ambassador in Washington, DC, His Excellency Mr. Faik Konitza. All enquiries will be treated in the strictest confidence.

There were surprisingly few takers.

Time was flying. Finally, some good news came from somewhere. His minions had found a Hungarian royal willing to take on the job. Zog did not know a thing about the Hungarians, so he likely read up. He was encouraged. Yes, there was once a massive kingdom, the biggest in central Europe, that they had ruled until the 1500s. Like Albania, they too were overrun by the Ottomans. They later reluctantly joined forces with the Habsburgs, and they were Christians, mostly Catholic, since the year 1000. Things got even better. Desperate to get territory back, they were Hitler's best ally. A Hungarian bride opened a door to Hitler and a potential exit from Mussolini's hold. Like the Albanians, their language was different, and they were surrounded by enemies. A totally unique people—just like the Albanians. Very encouraging, Zog must have thought.

Some Hungarians had fought the Ottomans alongside Skanderbeg in the 1400s. Geraldine claimed to be related to the original seven Hungarian tribes who arrived in Europe from Central Asia. Zog also lied about his lineage when he claimed to be a descendant of Skanderbeg. She was half American, 22 years younger than Zog, and beautiful but not rich by any means. He must have poured over the photos. He was certainly told they called her the "White Rose of Hungary." Hungary was like Albania, he was told, a mostly feudal place ruled by a backward and nostalgic aristocracy in weird furs and hats eager to keep things the way they always were—the perfect match. The peasants got the iron hand there too. It got better. They hated communists or anything on the left. Better still, Hungary was allied completely with Hitler. Zog saw some advantages to getting closer to Hitler in a roundabout way to balance his dependency on Mussolini. He certainly revisited the idea of reading *Mein Kampf* and writing a letter to Hitler. Zog's advisors had warned him about marrying someone from an important country, lest he drag Albania into nasty international politics. Hungary hardly mattered at all—the perfect outcome. There was a downside, though. He had to give up his good luck charm, Franzi.

Zog, Geraldine and Zog's sisters, 1939 in Sweden
Source: Wikimedia Commons

Geraldine arrived in Albania in late December 1937, and Zog proposed on New Year's Day 1938. She later said Zog had a great sense of humor, although the world knew little of this. Mussolini, on the other hand, was known to be funny. He once called Switzerland a republic of sausages and said Hitler was a gramophone with just seven tunes that he played repeatedly. The wedding was set for April. Trouble ensued when the Vatican said they would not sanction it unless Zog gave a written promise that any children would be raised as Catholics. Zog declined, but Ciano saved the day by intervening with the Pope, or at least he said he did. In any case, it was to be a civil service over in minutes, even though Geraldine had said she could manage becoming a Muslim. Zog promised to build his bride a Catholic chapel in the Royal Palace.

Despite the promise of a bride in 1938, things in Europe were changing quickly in ways Zog could not fathom. The states that largely came about as a result of the post-war peace treaties made in Paris in 1919–1920 found themselves facing extinction. Germany's borders to the West were acknowledged but those to the East were up for grabs. After bullying and interfering in Austrian political life since coming to power and admonishing the Austrian leadership for constant treachery and betrayal, Hitler annexed the place entirely in mid-March 1938. Hitler thus made good on his promise to start bringing all the Germans into one state. Plus, he satisfied his hatred of Austria and Vienna especially for its rejection of him prior to the First World War. After the invasion, which was met with no resistance, Hitler held a rigged plebiscite where more than 99 percent of voters agreed to Austria's disappearance. If many Austrians would not accept the end of Austria, they would at least embrace Hitler for his willingness to deal with the Jews in the same way he had done in Germany. That Mussolini let Austria go without a fight resulted in not just Hitler's undying gratitude but emboldened Mussolini's own plans for territorial revision and terrified Zog at the same time.

Prior to this, Zog tried in the strangest of ways to find allies outside of Italy. In February 1938, three of his unmarried sisters—Maxhide, Ruhije, and Myzejen—set sail for the United States ostensibly to collect wedding gifts for their future sister-in-law, but the papers all concluded they came to America to find rich husbands. This was the very first time the sisters had left Albania. Royal life had become stultifyingly dull, and, in some ways, they looked back on a better life as barefoot villagers. But since the Vienna incident, Zog could not leave Albania and never hesitated to use his sisters or other emissaries to promote his agenda. Zog was truly desperate for allies, so he must have told the sisters to make the right impression on the Americans.

Moreover, the sisters were expected to make an overture to the exiled Bishop Fan Noli at his church in Boston. In Boston, Noli held a special mass, and the sisters were there. The whole trip was a disaster, as the sisters were dubbed less than chic and very imperious by the media. They cancelled most of their events and sulked in the hotel room. Before long, they were on the Queen Mary headed for London and then Paris to do some shopping. During their American tour, Austria disappeared, but they hardly noticed, and nobody told them anyway.

Back in Albania, Zog was not thinking about Austria, as he had the wedding on his mind. Hitler and Mussolini were both invited to the wedding, along with a plethora of world leaders. No one of significance would come. Both Hitler and Mussolini declined to attend in person, but the two probably had a few giggles about the right gift.

When the wedding was announced in January for April 25, 1938, things in Europe were getting darker. But unlike his sisters, circumstances forced a panicked Zog to start thinking when Hitler abruptly ended Austrian independence in March 1938. Not only did he love Austria, but it gave him a reason to fear that if Hitler could make Austria simply disappear without a word from anyone, what could Mussolini get away with vis-à-vis Albania? Hopefully, the Hungarians could help.

Despite a gloomy international scene, the wedding went off in quiet Albania almost without a hitch. Geraldine's trousseau had been prepared by Hedi Raab, a Jewish dressmaker in Vienna who could not get a passport from Austria's new Nazi rulers, and Geraldine almost had to go without some sporting costumes. Hedi did not give up easily. She had an invite and a signed portrait of Geraldine that she presented to the Nazi gatekeepers, who let her go to Albania. Bereft of decent friends in Albania, the key witness for Zog was Count Ciano. It was 1928 all over again as Tirana was awash in flags, high society, mountaineers, and Italian military personnel who joined the parade down the city's one boulevard— the usual mix of east meets west. Italian planes flew overhead. A procession of cars made its way through the streets as stray dogs and cats looked on. The crowd threw flowers. The papers reported that the fierce northern tribesmen mingled with their hated barefoot brethren from the south and shared wine skins before returning to their routine of tribal warfare. The sisters and everyone else that mattered looked on, gave the fascist salute, and examined the masses below with total contempt. The wedding service in the relatively new Royal Palace had to be a civil one because of the religious differences. It lasted less than five minutes and Albania had a queen. In the photos, the only person who seemed to be smiling was Ciano, as though a baby filling a diaper. His sanguine look was his alone to know why, but one can conclude that Ciano was eager to tell his father-in-law that the Albanian plan was proceeding beautifully. Sitting on their new thrones, Zog and Geraldine received homage from the masses. A new stamp, showing Geraldine and a much younger-looking Zog, was issued in case anyone mailed a letter.

The train of Geraldine's white satin gown was carried by Prince Tati, who was old enough to know that his days as heir apparent were numbered if the king and queen decided to have sex. Zog had his saber and his medals on full display. Geraldine brought her favorite Gypsy band from Hungary for the reception, and they played all her favorites. She cut the wedding cake with Zog's sword. The streets were covered with slogans that foreshadowed the communist passion for slogans plastered everywhere: Viva King Zog, Viva Duce. There was the Italian fascist salute too. The peasants could hardly be expected to know what was next. The glitter of Tirana had not made it to the villages. Coarse bread and cheese were on the menu. Twenty-eight other couples decided to marry the same day, and Zog foot the bill. Ever practical, Geraldine was kind enough to buy each couple a mattress, blanket, and pillows. Some likely asked for cash instead.

The gifts were odd. Of course, Zog got his wife a diamond tiara. Hitler sent an open-topped scarlet and supercharged Mercedes 540K. Interestingly, King Farouk of Egypt got the same one when he married his first wife in January 1938. The car type must have been cursed. Zog would end up in exile in King Farouk's Egypt in 1946, and King Farouk would also end up in exile in Italy in 1952. As to Mussolini's gift, he sent some gilded bronze vases that allegedly once belonged to Napoleon—given to the "Napoleon of the Balkans." Horthy sent china from the famous Hungarian Herend Company, but another Hungarian notable sent horses and a carriage. Prime Minister Winston Churchill sent nothing. Turkey sent rugs. After the ceremony, they set off in the new car to their new palace in Durres as the barefoot peasants lined the road to cheer them on. In the absence of big guests besides Ciano, Zog and Geraldine had to make do with long-forgotten royalty from Hungary whose days were as numbered as theirs. Zog did not smile in a single photo.

A weird tragedy followed the wedding. Zog decided that some of the gifts he received could be returned for cash in Paris and Vienna. He sent more than 1 million dollars in gifts, including some jewelry he decided not to buy, on a plane that included several of the attendees from the wedding on a flight from Tirana to Brindisi to Rome. On the Brindisi-Rome leg of the journey, the plane crashed in the Maranola Mountains north of Naples and 19 people died, including Albania's ambassador in Rome, an Italian archaeologist, a Nazi journalist, and a *Newsweek* correspondent. The jewelry was never recovered but it was insured. Apparently, the heat of the crash melted everything. The bodies were quickly grabbed by the local fascists who arrived on the scene.

Ciano's diaries hardly record a mention of the wedding, only to say that the ceremony "passed off with more dignity than one might have expected" and that the population was "indifferent" and more "ragged than usual." In a report to his father-in-law, Ciano referred to "the most uncivilized Balkan court" and noted that the court seemed "grotesque if we consider the social stature and habits of its members." Ciano's hatred of Zog was based on class: Ciano was nobility, Zog was not. Ciano referred to Zog as "a bandit" and "the so-called king." Ciano lamented having to go to provincial Tirana, which was not London or Paris. However, Ciano's dismissal of the whole event masked the fact that both at the ceremony and after he felt slighted. According to those present, Zog's sisters ignored him and were even overheard complaining about Italy's role in Albania. Ciano concluded that Zog was attempting to move Albania into Hitler's sphere of influence. The link would be Geraldine's pro-German Hungarian family, who had so openly supported Austria's annexation. Ciano was even more convinced when Zog made such a show of driving off to the palace in Durres in the Mercedes Hitler had sent. Immediately after the wedding, Ciano had started to plot to have Zog assassinated. He later shelved the plan to invade in favor of just simply booting Zog out.

The fate of places like Albania became even more precarious by the fall of 1938, when Hitler re-ordered the map twice. After applying nearly the same tactics in the German-inhabited areas of Czechoslovakia as he did in Austria, he was handed those territories for the sake of world peace in September 1938 in Munich. The Czechs were hardly consulted, but they must have been relieved to have the Germans out of their country. However, the partition of Czechoslovakia ushered in a new era, as it was quickly followed by Hitler-sponsored territorial revisions in Hungary's favor in November. In Albania, Zog was doing his best to mimic Mussolini to stave off an invasion. He made his sister Myzejen patroness of sports who led a group of female gymnasts doing the Mussolini salute. To celebrate the tenth anniversary of the kingdom, Zog had a weird monument to liberty built.

By March 1939, Hitler ended the state of Czechoslovakia by seizing Bohemia and Moravia, turning them into a German protectorate and setting up an independent Slovakia as a puppet state eager to do the Germans' bidding. The post-war order was overturned completely.

In the world of 1939, Zog had no idea what to do. He abhorred the madness of Hitler—he read the speeches and watched the newsreels. But jealousy did persist in the way any dictator envies the power of another. But compared to him, Hitler was low level—Zog was a colonel and a king, who fought in multiple wars. Hitler was a mere corporal. Zog readily bought the anti-Bolshevik stuff, but the attack on the Jews had always been beyond his comprehension.

Italy was a bigger problem. Italy had to invade Albania if only to keep up with the Germans and Mussolini was fed up with Hitler's *fait accomplis*. Despite a near total lack of information, Zog sensed something was afoot that could well send him packing. In March 1939, Zog sent Chatin Sarachi, of Bari and Vienna assassination fame, to London for talks with Winston Churchill to propose the neutralization of Albania in exchange for allowing Jewish refugees in. Sarachi informed Churchill that he was prepared to negotiate for the safety of the Jews. The talks never occurred, and Churchill

A somber Zog and stern Ciano, 1937. Source: AQSH (Central State Archive of Albania), photo collection of Ahmet Zog.

likely realized too late that Zog may well have been serious. By the time the offer made it to Churchill, the Italian plans had advanced too far.

By early 1939, Mussolini was totally despondent and acting childishly. In power since 1922, eleven years before Hitler, Mussolini grew frustrated with the role of sidekick. Every time Hitler occupied a country—Austria in March 1938, the Sudetenland of Czechoslovakia in November 1938, then all the Czech lands in March 1939—Mussolini fell into a deeper and deeper depression, fearing that the whole world was laughing at him. He would pay Hitler back, he told Ciano, with his own coin. There was always Albania, and the Italians had Zog over the proverbial barrel—they offered him some bad terms to disappear in the form of an ultimatum, which meant union with Italy and Zog's demotion to full-fledged puppet. When Zog declined, Mussolini invented spurious reasons to invade. By then, since border changes had become near normal, there was not much Albania could do. For the second time in 25 years, the country would disappear from the map of Europe. Zog knew it was coming despite the multiple friendship treaties he had signed with Mussolini. Italy had a ready excuse and Zog's days were numbered. As a poor planner, it is doubtful Zog knew this. It is likely that he hoped that Leka's birth would deter any adventurism on Italy's part.

With big lies the order of the day, Ciano claimed that Italian lives and interests were in danger and, more ridiculously, that Zog was planning to invade Yugoslavia. For the sake of peace, Ciano insisted, Zog had to go. The foreign diplomats all concluded that Zog, as slippery as he was, was not so reckless as to invade his northern neighbor. Others in the Italian government said Zog governed as a tyrannical feudal and greedy lord who neglected the needs of his people. The Italians would save them. Other lofty reasons were put forth as justifications: a Europe-wide recognition that Italian interests were preeminent there and given the global circumstances, Albania could not defend itself, and that the Italian community in Albania was endangered. Whatever good had happened in Albania, Mussolini insisted, was solely from Italian influence. On April 4, Queen Geraldine went into labor as Albania edged towards a real heir. On April 5, Albania had a male heir when Leka was born. Zog was busy packing up. On Good Friday, April 7, 1939, at the start of a nice long weekend when no one was looking and even the British Prime Minister Neville Chamberlain was on holiday in Scotland, 40,000 Italian troops invaded Albania at four coastal places. In keeping with the carnival-like atmosphere, Count Ciano flew his own plane there, landing at an airfield north of Tirana to congratulate the troops, pose for the photographers, wave to the rent-a-crowd shouting "Viva il Duce," and tour Zog's empty palace, where maybe he stole an ashtray from the Regina Hotel given to Zog by the Janka sisters.

Mussolini did not bother to come this time (he showed up in 1940 instead, when his army invaded Greece from Albania). On April 8, Zog got on the radio to talk to no one in particular. Looking out the window from the radio room, he could watch as the getaway cars were being loaded. It was hardly a Churchillian moment when he declared that he would fight until the last drop of blood was spilled. Shortly after the speech, Zog fled to avoid his hanging, which Mussolini had ordered for no apparent reason. Nobody in London or Paris seemed at all concerned about Zog or even Albania. The hasty departure did little to win him any allies later when he hoped to regain the throne. In the late 1930s, countries came and went. A few troops tried to hold the port of Durres until the ammunition ran out; otherwise, the Albanian army disintegrated. Chaos reigned in Tirana as, not for the first time in the twentieth century, a mob opened the prisons and released everyone while others looted the various royal homes of Zog and his sisters.

The whole thing was over in 48 hours as Albania fell easily despite the disastrous shortcomings of the Italian invasion. Seamlessly, Victor Emmanuel III became the King of Albania. Most Albanians, having endured so many changes in systems without a shred of real change, appeared indifferent to the arrival of another monarchy—their third since Wied. The Italians counted on Zog's easy capitulation. With a new wife and baby, Ciano never expected Zog to retreat à la Bajram Curri or Hasan Prishtina to the mountains to begin a prolonged struggle to regain his kingdom. The foreign diplomats concluded that while Zog had failed as a ruler, leaving little but apathy in his people, Albania hardly deserved to be invaded.

With the absorption of the Albanian Muslims into the growing Italian empire that included the Muslims in Africa, Mussolini pledged to build a mosque in Rome to show his inclusive side. The mosque never appeared. His project, Mussolini hoped, was not to be compared with the nasty Nazis, who were mere colonizers who destroyed nations. Italy, he proclaimed, was on a civilizing mission; the Albanian nation would be nurtured and brought up to a European standard. Albania was to become an Italian tourist destination. After all, the Albanians were known for their great hospitality. It was not a mission of destruction and the emptying of people to make room for Italians like the Germans were doing in Eastern Europe. Count Ciano, who set up the provisional government in Albania, was eager to convince the world that their empire, built on the foundations of the Roman Empire, was *sui generis* in its enlightened goals. Albania even got its very own fascist party and the façade of independence while the Italians plundered the place. Tirana got another makeover to accommodate a new House of Fascism and an Assembly Square adorned with statues celebrating ancient Rome. The Lana River separated colonizers from colonized, as the Italians built themselves stately villas on the south side, leaving the Albanians in "old" Tirana.

Queen Geraldine, in poor health, left first with the baby Leka and waited for Zog at the Greek-Albanian border. His escape routes were somewhat blocked. Italy was obviously not an option. He could not go to Belgrade again as the Serbs no longer had any use for him. This left only Greece. Zog fled in the supercharged Mercedes Hitler gave him as a wedding gift with an entourage of 100 people, heavily armed and firing into the air just for effect. They allegedly carried seven crates of gold weighing over 180 kilograms. Fearing Mussolini would murder him, the British helped Zog get out. But in one way, Zog had Mussolini to thank for the getaway, as he had built some roads to get ready to invade Greece from Albania. Much of Zog's wealth was portable, and he left Albania fantastically wealthy, despite later denials by his son. As an ironic reward for spending the money on himself instead of a road network, after driving out of Tirana through the towns of Lushnje, Fier, and Gjirokaster, the Mercedes was trashed and Zog sold it when he got to Greece. It took him two days to make the journey, and he did not even need to go incognito, as hardly a single person recognized him as he had never ever visited Albania's south. There were no spontaneous demonstrations along the way, but no doubt the locals were perplexed by the speeding scarlet convertible stirring up dust in the villages as it made its way south. "There goes another king," the few in the know must have thought.

Crossing into Greece on April 8, Zog went from pledging to fight to the last drop of blood to pledging his eventual return for the freedom fight. You cannot fault him for failing to realize that he would never set foot on Albanian soil again. He issued another radio appeal from Greece urging his people to fight, but in a country with so few radios, nobody heard anything. Zog's departure was hardly noticed for obvious reasons. Who could know that in the next five years Albania would see full-fledged Italian occupation, German occupation, a brutal civil war, and the triumph of what would become Europe's weirdest communists.

In places where rulers can change often and jubilation is often required from weary peasants, within 24 hours of Zog's departure, almost overnight Tirana was awash in Italian flags and the fascist Roman salute, which was no different than the Zogist salute. Tellingly, the only places destroyed by mobs were Zog's palaces. One former ally of Zog declared that since Albanians could not govern themselves, they simply needed Mussolini to save them from further disasters. Barely a week after, Albanian notables, led by

Zog's one-time prospective father-in-law, Shefket Vërlaci, arrived personally in Rome and offered the Albanian throne, such as it was, to the very frail Victor Emmanuel III. This was an extremely special and proud moment for Vërlaci, who almost immediately issued an order for Zog to be assassinated. The charge: national embarrassment. Spurning his daughter and sullying the family honor had to have a price according to the Kanun and just plain revenge. Old scores had to be settled. In other more mundane news, a few days later, Albania (and Hungary) withdrew from the League of Nations and the Nazis moved to ban "pernicious" music.

Chapter Nine

Meanwhile, in Albania

After fleeing Albania, Zog and the royal entourage moved from place to place. First, they went to Greece, where they were not especially welcome in what was then a kind of fascist but pro-British state that preferred not to talk about Albania for fear of upsetting the Duce. The Greeks had long worried not just about Mussolini's Roman Empire dreams but also about his claims on what was once the Venetian Empire, which included parts of Greece, including Corfu.

From Greece, Zog went to Turkey, then Romania, then Poland, then Sweden. He even visited the Baltic States before they disappeared in the pact between Stalin and Hitler in August 1939. In 1940, the family moved to France, where they rented mansions before taking up residence in the Hotel Plaza Athénée, just off Paris's Champs-Elysée. With the defeat of France, Zog left for the UK, where he and his family spent much of the war in London's Ritz Hotel with other exiled Balkan royalty.

Since the UK had offered Zog asylum as long as he stayed out of politics, by November 1944, Zog was just a country gentleman in Parmoor House in Frieth in the United Kingdom, waiting for a bored journalist to come to make fun of him. He walked to the local pub in a country gentleman's outfit to get more cigarettes. In Albania, the communist forces were gaining the upper hand with extraordinary support from the UK. Given the UK's commitment, Zog was totally sidelined, and Churchill never met him.

The Italian occupation collapsed in 1943 with Italy signing an armistice with the Allies. The German Army took over in 1943. Stretched too thin by then, the Germans avoided a full-scale occupation but instead opted for a neutral, pro-German Albania run by some of the usual landowning suspects from the Zog era. The Albanians under German occupation got off easy to a degree, especially when compared to neighboring Greece and Yugoslavia.

To the great credit of the Albanian people, the fate of the Jews there tells an altogether positive story in a century that until then had provided mostly misery and failure. While Zog had only reluctantly imposed anti-Jewish laws in 1938 at Mussolini's insistence, they went unimplemented in the way that any law was applied by Balkan standards. The Italian occupation authorities found the Albanians unwilling to take any steps towards rounding up Jews. According to later orders from the Italians, they were to observe the Jews but not punish them. The Albanians did neither. In fact, Albanians of all three religions did their best to shelter Jews under the Albanian tradition of *Besa*, which meant that a guest had to be protected. The Germans also found the Albanians unwilling to hand over any lists of Jews either. Some 2000 Jews, largely fleeing the German occupation of Yugoslavia that began in 1941, found safety in Albania. Even in exile, Zog had tried to exploit the fate of the Jews to facilitate his return to Albania. He met with the Anglo-Jewish community and extolled the virtues of the Jews as potential saviors of Albania, emphasizing that the Jews had capital and that Jews and Albanians had a shared legacy of persecution. In exile, Zog again offered 150,000 hectares of land, largely swampland that needed to be drained, that would accommodate, according to him, 50,000 families. The plan collapsed because Zog made the offer contingent on getting the throne back. On that, he was not prepared to negotiate. Zog was livid when he learned that some Jews had settled in the Dominican Republic under the tyrant Rafael Trujillo, who was also eager to sanitize his murderous image. Nevertheless, by the end of the war, nearly one hundred percent of Jews in Albania survived the war, making Albania unique in Europe as having a larger Jewish population after the war than before.

In extremely bitter warfare, Albanian communists fought the Italians, the Germans, German collaborators, and Zog's few supporters. By the end of

November 1944, Zog got very bad news. The communists, who under Enver Hoxha's leadership were clever enough to hide under the guise of the National Liberation Front, "liberated" Tirana and the Germans withdrew as they hardly wanted to be there in the first place. Hoxha was a charismatic and brilliant organizer with impeccable credentials. After being kicked out of school in Montpellier in 1931, Hoxha went to Paris where he spent some time writing polemics against Zog under the pseudonym Lulo Malesori and making periodic pilgrimages to the site where Rustemi gunned down Esad Pasha. He later worked at the Albanian consulate in Brussels before returning to Albania to devote himself full-time to a communist revolution. Fired as a schoolteacher for refusing to join the Fascist party, his tobacco kiosk in Tirana became the go-to spot for would-be revolutionaries. The CIA had to acknowledge that he was "handsome, unreliable, cunning, ruthless, and possessed of a driving ambition." The Italian authorities issued an arrest warrant and sentenced him to death in absentia in 1941.

When Hoxha and his partisans entered Tirana, a new era, even an epoch, had begun, promising social justice and the total destruction of Zog's quasi-feudal order. Their entry into Tirana was perfectly choreographed to indicate that they were simply the people's choice. If the worst place to start a socialist revolution had been Russia in 1917, agrarian, nonindustrial, and uneducated Albania was even worse, at least as far as Marx would have seen things. But Albania's communists did not really have to tell big lies—who could deny that the preceding 25 years had been horrible? The party promised a march on the path of socialist transformation thanks entirely to Joseph Stalin, the savior of mankind, according to the new party line.

The communists could now turn their attention to the internal opposition, the so-called reactionary elements, to lay the groundwork for a totally new socialist order. Vengeance was the order of the day everywhere the communists took power. In 1946, Zog's monarchy was abolished and Albania became a People's Republic. Special courts, led by Koçi Xoxe, were soon established where charges of collaboration with Zog, the Italians, or the Germans got an immediate death sentence. Thousands of others faced torture and imprisonment. While all communist takeovers were violent, the Albanian one stood out for the sheer number of executions—estimated at 6,000 between 1944 and 1991. The communists promised free elections, just like everywhere in Eastern Europe. But when votes did come, voters had only one list that contained people with good communist credentials or reliable fellow travelers. In the first election, the communists took over 90 percent of the vote. Albania skipped the period of sham democracy on offer in Hungary or Czechoslovakia. Albanians knew the system had always been rigged and would stay rigged.

The vagaries of intra-party life, with its regular bloodletting and outrageous fabrications of epic betrayal by even top party bosses, and the chaotic world of international communism determined Albania's trajectory in the most bizarre ways. It was, in weird ways, a kind of family affair, a triumvirate of sorts, as Hoxha, Xoxe, and Mehmet Shehu joined their wives in launching Albania into this new era. A new royal court, complete with some family ties and just as tiny as Zog's, was in place. Hoxha's wife, Nexhmije, assumed an outsized role in the new regime. She had proven herself an ardent opponent of Zog and later the Italian occupation forces. Like her husband, she had a reputation for ruthlessness. With a new, albeit red, dynasty in power, the people entered a permanent fog, as it was never clear just what was going on. Like most communists in power in Europe, the mediocrity of the people in power was astonishing, saying as much about them as it did about the people they ruled over. Outside the narrow and predatory elite, everyone else grew accustomed to fear and poverty. Poverty was hardly new, but permanent fear was.

Hoxha also wanted to abolish the old tribal laws of the *Kanun* of Lek, which he viewed as reactionary and an obstacle to Stalinist modernity. Blood vengeance did not die, though; it was merely taken over by the government or went underground. Nobody could tell the difference anyway between blood vengeance and party vengeance. Hoxha went after the clan system too. Tribal leaders in the north faced humiliation, as in addition to being arrested, beaten, and tortured, they were paraded around their villages. Putting peasants on collective farms and piling people into poorly built housing blocks helped. Arranged marriages were forbidden and, at least on paper, patriarchy ended; Albania's women were liberated. But the feuds persisted, especially in the north. Other feuds just got buried and waited, just like Zog, for the end of communism to make everything that was old new again. Nothing would be forgotten or forgiven, but the communists needed to stay ahead of the curve as repression wound up necessitating more repression. In England, Zog apparently vowed to kill himself. It was a bluff. The exiled court had heard it all before. In any case, Zog's Albania was about to become unrecognizable.

Hoxha was arguably the only intellectual of the communist leaders to take power throughout what became Eastern Europe. By communist leader standards in the Balkans, Hoxha was quite educated, knew his Marxism-Leninism and Stalinism, and had even traveled a bit in Western Europe. Hoxha understood that Albanians had been derided as hopelessly divided—in Marxism-Leninism-Stalinism, Hoxha felt he had found the basis for unity. Almost seamlessly, Albania slid easily from one form of dictatorship to another.

For parties that claimed to represent the working class, hardly anybody actually came from the working class. In terms of the governments that emerged, there was far more continuity than most people at first realized. Most other leaders who were put in place by the Soviets were nothing more than "school of hard knocks" types or wily peasants who represented a tiny fraction of the population. But Albania's communist takeover was different, and the communists largely had Zog to thank for that. It was the poorest and least developed country in Europe. Albania's communists had also done it without the Red Army. In Budapest, Bucharest, Prague, Sofia, and Warsaw the Red Army made communism possible and essentially kept it there for the next four decades. Albania (and Yugoslavia) was an outlier and that gave the communists some special credentials—a particular passion for homegrown violence but also some legitimacy. They could not have defeated their opponents otherwise.

That Albania's illiterate peasants got in line to swear allegiance to another despot made total sense. The Albania that the communists took over was the least developed country in Europe and illiteracy was over 80 percent. Zog had built very few schools. The communists certainly raced to change that, especially since religious schools had until then been the key educators. That had to end. Once the communists taught the people to read, most of them easily adjusted to swallowing the vacant slogans and the intricacies of Marxism-Leninism-Stalinism that were to come from the communists, just the same as they did when they swallowed Zog's sham monarchy with its faux court life and dazzling princesses in western dress. Where Zog had never said a word, the communists never shut up. One could also easily understand why the people might be perplexed. A middle-aged person had witnessed by then the end of the Ottoman Empire, an independent Albania, violent wars waged on Balkan Muslims, a German king, a parliamentary republic, a presidential republic, an Albanian king, then an Italian one, and then a German occupation. The only thread was misery. Embracing something that might put paid to that past was welcome. Everything else had failed. Nobody could question that. In those circumstances, trying something new made total sense.

In terms of setting up another, albeit different, dictatorship in Albania, Hoxha had lots of options to choose from, but the obvious choice even without the Red Army and its secret police on Albanian territory was Stalinism. As Hoxha saw the world, only Stalinism offered a gateway to the modernity and real independence that had evaded Albania. A country of olive groves, sheep, goats, and fruit was hardly his vision. Albania had to be industrial and only the USSR under Stalin had achieved this. Zog's feudal ruling elite made hasty exits or ended up in jails, dead, or in internal exile. They were rounded up, thrown out of their villas, and sent for reeducation. Borders were eventually closed, making escape nearly impossible. Albania's beautiful Adriatic coast was to become a heavily fortified military zone. The narrow strip of sea that separated Albania from the Greek island of Corfu became a death trap. Any attempt to flee was punishable by death, either at the hands of shoot-to-kill orders given to border guards or execution after a rigged trial. Albania drifted towards a highly militarized society where everyone was deemed a soldier. The inner circle, living lavishly by local standards, grew increasingly paranoid. Insecure in their grip on power, outside influences were curtailed and then banned altogether.

Zog's "feudal and bloodthirsty regime," according to the communists, aided and abetted by the Italian fascists, had enslaved the Albanians, or so the Albanians were told. Land reform finally came when Albania's seven great landowning families saw their property nationalized. The peasants were herded onto collective or state farms where most products went to the state, leaving meager remains for them. As Stalin had done, agricultural goods were to be sold for hard currency to build a modern state. Rationing was the key. The diet of bread and cheese continued unabated. There was no electricity outside of the few cities and no indoor plumbing. The communists, eager to create a new and loyal communist citizenry, taught people how to read with a crash anti-illiteracy drive. How else could you read the slogans promising a world of plenty by harnessing agriculture and new industry? The peasants went to the mountainsides once more to arrange the white rocks with spontaneous slogans extolling the party, its achievements, and its leader. They were promised electricity and proper apartments. Secret police were another must, alongside an ever-expanding list of snitches eager to advance in the new world at the expense of a better-off neighbor or family member. It was a new world of constant surveillance. People queued to get new jobs with a modest office and a typewriter. If, under Zog, a coveted state job required a payment to a third-tier bureaucrat or some furtive sex, a new currency was now in place. Party loyalists paid with information on class enemies or people with bad biographies. A single newspaper, *Voice of the People*, told the story of Albania's internal and external enemies, along with a growing list of people sent to death or forced labor. In 1948, the Russians, this time the Red ones, came again but this time as advisors with cash to help make Albania an industrial powerhouse. They helped establish a Stalin City that was built with prison labor and would house a base for Soviet warplanes. A Stalin Textile Mill, Karl Marx Hydroelectric power station, and a Lenin Cement Plant all followed.

But at first, with loads of help from neighboring Yugoslavia, Hoxha set out to create an entirely new national narrative. He maintained that the Albanians had hacked their way through history as empires came and went and neighbors sought to destroy them, which set the stage for Albania's isolation. This narrative spoke of encirclement and dangerous Western imperialism, led largely by the United States, which was determined to destroy Albania's independence. Zog's murdered enemies, like Curri, Gurakuqi, and Rustemi, got streets, squares, or towns named after them as new heroes quickly replaced the old ones. Hoxha went after any competing center of loyalty. Zog's legacy was easy to erase. He had done so little that it took hardly any effort to make it seem as though he was never there. He disappeared like the morning mist. Besides, the Italian occupiers had already started the process of Zog's erasure. The communists kept the few palaces and the Italian-built ministry buildings, and the grand boulevard quickly became Stalin Boulevard.

Religious tolerance was out as Albania was set to take secularism to a whole new level. Albania's three religions came under vicious attack by party militants. Hoxha focused on the Catholics first, fearing the Vatican was simply too dangerous. Hoxha claimed the Church had collaborated with the Italians and opposed communist rule, which was true. Their schools were closed, property seized, and the clergy jailed, sent to forced labor, or executed. Ultimately, any form of religious expression was to be eliminated as the ultimate poison, the proverbial opium of the people that had enslaved them. The communists rounded up the Jesuits, charged them with spying for the Americans, and shot them in a cemetery. In March 1948 alone, 19 clergy were tortured then executed. Those that survived prison ended up as public toilet cleaners to be humiliated. Before long, the country's largest Catholic cathedral would become a sports palace. Religious leaders were invited to start a dialogue about ensuring their allegiance to the new order, only to be tricked, lied to, and then simply shot.

Proving your loyalty had no limits in the dog-eat-dog world of Albanian communism. The hated Catholic clergy had to go. Local militants in Albania's north did some grave robbing and removed the bones of a famous Franciscan priest with a bad biography. They threw his remains in a local river to finish him off completely. The young militants were destined for great things, having shown both vision and spontaneity. Medals were awarded, rations increased, and blossoming careers were promised, where vigilance towards the dangerous class enemies was required.

Life inside the party was just as dangerous as Hoxha saw enemies everywhere. A struggle was brewing over Albania's future direction and its relations with Yugoslavia. In November 1947, Albanians learned that Nako Spiru, their 29-year-old minister of the economy and industry, died while playing with a revolver in his office. Later, the story changed—he had killed himself out of remorse for leading the party astray.

Chapter Ten

One Last Chance

In the world of international affairs, there are times when small states can punch far above their weight, and in 1948, Albania started to matter. Prior to that, even the US had decided that Albania was strategically insignificant. Events in neighboring communist Yugoslavia were about to change not just Albania's fate but that of the entire Stalinist bloc of communist states. Those opened possibilities. Yugoslavia's leader, Josip Broz "Tito," accumulated too much power for Stalin's liking by pursuing regional ambitions that ran counter to Stalin's vision of total control. With Albanian acquiescence, there was real talk of Albania joining Yugoslavia. Even during the war, Albania had hardly been mentioned, and so its attachment to Yugoslavia seemed almost natural. Nako Spiru had opposed the plan and now he was dead.

Hoxha found himself in a bit of a pickle. What side to be on? He later gauged which way the wind was blowing and eventually sided with Stalin, and decisively made Albania the most Stalinist country in the bloc. These were precarious times for Hoxha; he could have easily ended up on the wrong side of history with a bullet in his head. Stalin, in fact, had no fondness for Hoxha, having despised intellectual communists from the beginning. The pro-Yugoslav faction in Albania faced swift justice. Hoxha's number two man, an allegedly illiterate tinsmith and thus a real proletarian, Koçi Xoxe, who had overseen, as minister of the interior, the violent communization process, was later charged as a Western spy and a tool of Tito aspiring to turn Albania into Tito's colony.

Xoxe was the typical fall guy for a regime that badly needed scapegoats. He went quickly from a grand office with a view of Skanderbeg Square to a basement cell with a peephole in the same building. He was regularly tortured and interrogated by former friends. After performing some vile self-criticism where he confessed to everything, including spying for Zog and Tito and pledging undying fealty to Enver in the totally futile attempt to save his life, Xoxe was summarily executed in June 1949. His last testament, in the form of a letter to Hoxha, was from a man who knew he had to die for the sake of the party. His allies and family were banished to prisons or internal exile with permanent bad biographies. Rumors persisted that he had been strangled in a politburo meeting by Mehmet Shehu. Xoxe was the first in what was to become a long line of executed interior ministers in the years to come. In a way that was to become typical, Nako Spiru was right all along, so the once disgraced party member was removed from his unmarked grave, reburied somewhere more fitting, and restored to the pantheon of communist greats—at least until the next change in course.

For those that survived, there was no way back to the fold. Bad biographies did not often disappear. The message to the ordinary Albanian following the lurid evidence of the trial could only be fear and bewilderment. Xoxe's death unleashed a wave of internal party violence and not just in Albania. If the number two of the party could be sent to death, how could anyone survive short of total obedience? Albania became the most devoted of all Stalin's satellites, but the break with Yugoslavia left Albania geographically vulnerable. Stalin embraced the Albanians and sent assassins to murder Tito. They failed. But Stalin did save Albania, and Albania had a new number two man: Mehmet Shehu. A largely uneducated but devoted communist, veteran of the Garibaldi international brigade in the Spanish Civil War, and an extremely able military commander during Albania's liberation war, Shehu would develop a reputation for extraordinary ruthlessness and brutality. He would take over the dark deeds file.

The evolving order and its perceived instability gave Zog another chance. After all, he did expel the "Red Bishop" in 1924, and maybe he could do it again. He had the credentials to topple the now isolated Albanian communists. Based on a generous offer from Egypt's royal family, Zog and his family arrived in Egypt, allegedly with 2000 pieces of luggage, in February 1946 to a very warm welcome from King Farouk and his wife, Farida, and rooms with a view of the pyramids. The Egyptian Court was extremely lavish, corrupt, and filled with lots of other out-of-work monarchs from Bulgaria and Italy. Ironically, since Victor Emmanuel III of Italy was there too, there were technically two kings of Albania in Egypt. The Italian King allegedly apologized to Zog for stealing his kingdom in 1939. It was all Mussolini's idea anyway, he must have claimed.

Farouk and Zog made for an unlikely pair. In Zog, Farouk found a card-playing partner. Oddly, given that Zog came from the poorest country, given how he spent money, he appeared to be the wealthiest of all. Egypt's King Farouk, whose days were numbered, liked having them around, and the spies of the UK and the US sought Zog out to plot ways to turn the tables on the communists. In Egypt, things started to look up for Zog. He first tried to resurrect his Muslim credentials to rally the support of the Muslim world for a crusade against the godless Albanian communists. The Muslim world, not for the last time either, decided not to help the Albanians.

But in the West, Zog could get few sympathetic ears until everything changed. The Berlin Blockade of 1948–49, an early crisis in the emerging Cold War when Stalin attempted to shut the Western airlines out of their enclave in Berlin, had enraged the West. Earlier in 1948, Czechoslovakia, by then the only country in Eastern Europe that had not been completely Sovietized, fell to the communists in a bizarre coup in February. Eastern Europe was lost, but at that moment, many hoped the communist grip was only tentative. The Americans were the first to consider active intervention to foster discontent. The Albanian break with Tito meant Albania was cut off, surrounded by enemies, and maybe ripe for the taking. Just as important, the Americans concluded that 90 percent of Albanians were against the communists. The West needed an easy victory, and Albania seemed like low-hanging fruit. Albania would become the target of the first attempt to topple a communist government.

1949 proved to be another grim year for the anti-communist world. North Korea fell to communism and China headed in the same direction. By December 1949, the UK's Secret Intelligence Service started serious work in Albania after canvassing for ideas on how to secure a victory there while also aiding the Greeks in the struggle against communist forces. British Prime Minister Clement Atlee came up with an easy plan: surely the Albanian communists were for sale, so he suggested paying them. That aside, it was simply assumed to be the weakest link in the communist chain, and this led to wildly inaccurate assessments of the internal situation. Albania was a great experiment in a new world—the ultimate bridgehead for subversive activities designed to split the Eastern Bloc, weaken Moscow's influence, and conclusively remove the communist presence from the Adriatic Sea. But how? They would engage Zog, who wildly exaggerated his influence and the Albanian desire to see him back, train exiled Albanians, drop them covertly into Albania, and let them foment an uprising and murder the communist leaders, and that would be that. It would be easy. It had the added benefit of hindering Albania's communists from aiding their ideological soul mates in Greece's civil war. It would embolden resistance movements everywhere. It was irresistible. They just needed volunteers. Hundreds of Albanian emigrants were trained at a secret base in Malta. It could not be any easier. Worst case scenario, it would start a civil war, like in neighboring Greece, and force the USSR to divert resources there to prop up the Albanian communists. The British took the plan to the US and asked them to help bring down the Hoxha government and the US was enthusiastic. The US was more than willing to foot the bill. Operation Valuable, as it was known in the United Kingdom, and Operation Fiend, in the US, was launched in 1949. In their overly optimistic situation reports, they judged Albania as essentially weak and unstable, and that most of the population was close to starving. If Albania fell, everything was possible. A few were skeptical and worried that an Albanian intervention could go the other way if the USSR intervened with real force to save its only foothold on the Adriatic Sea.

Zog had a head start on everyone plotting to topple the communists. In September 1947, he sent representatives to Washington and London, proposing that they work together to overthrow the Communist regime in Albania. Of course, he also wanted recognition of his crown and financial support for his exiled entourage. At this time, the British seemed sympathetic but did not consider the moment opportune for a move against

Hoxha. Zog was gracious with his offers: propaganda, sabotage, and intelligence from both Albania and Yugoslavia. Zog burnished his arguments with his rudimentary understanding of Marxism, holding forth on how it could never work in Albania. Because he had left the country feudal, Albania could not be communist, he argued. The CIA and SIS decided they were not interested. Zog and his supporters, they concluded, had limited abilities and were overstating their access. And thus, in late 1948, the programs, as conceived by the British, had a minimum and maximum objective. The maximum objective was to dislodge Albania from the Soviet sphere, thus denying the Soviets their prized Mediterranean access and, even more importantly, inspiring other Central and East European Communist countries to break away from the Iron Curtain. A minimum objective was simply to show they were doing something and to chip away at the regime over the long haul. 1947 had other problems though that suggested to Zog that time was running short for a comeback. In November 1947, the future Queen Elizabeth II married Philip Mountbatten of the Greek royal family. Out of work royals from Romania and Yugoslavia were there. Zog was not invited. He was certainly furious. What had he done to deserve this?

In what were new and promising circumstances after the break with Yugoslavia, in 1949, the British and the Americans began talking to Zog in Cairo and Alexandria. The initial meetings in May and June—which included top spies from the US and UK—took place in Zog's villa in Alexandria. There too was Kim Philby, who would later be outed as one of the USSR's key assets in British intelligence, and the failures in Albania would largely be blamed on him, although there were other problems. According to Queen Geraldine, she had a sense that there was something not quite right about Philby. Zog, who demanded to be called his majesty, held forth about his legions of supporters, the hate for the regime among all Albanians, and the desire for his return. His servants still bowed and retreated from the room backwards. He brought out all the tropes and cliches of 1928—Albanians had spontaneously begged to be a kingdom; a kingdom was the natural order of things for the ever-hierarchical Albanians, who simply had to swear fealty to a king. He had brought the Albanians, kicking and screaming, into Europe by banishing Islam and creating the foundation for a modern and

Western state. He built a few roads. The spies said they also wanted a democratic Albania, which perplexed Zog, although he nevertheless concurred. He fell back on his usual mantra: he had made Albania and he would decide its future. His British interlocutors wondered how successful they could be in an uprising given that everyone knew Zog was a reactionary. Zog was brought on board when he was promised a referendum on the monarchy once Albania had been liberated.

The first phase of the plan consisted of forming a committee that would bring together the anti-communist opposition in exile. That was no easy task as the only thing the Albanians in exile had in common was hatred of communism. In the next stage, propaganda activities would soften up the Albanian regime. The key stage was training the emigre Albanians—also known as "Pixies"—to infiltrate Albania. (They were called Pixies because the Americans and British found them to be quite short.) Propaganda would start with the announcement of the new committee and Albanian-language radio broadcasts in Athens, Thessaloniki, and possibly Ankara telling any Albanians who could listen that an anti-communist resistance was forming. Listening to foreign broadcasts or owning a radio without registering it was a guarantee of a lengthy prison sentence. Hardly anyone even owned a radio, and buying one required a permit. The CIA thought about sending disposable radios for the peasants but thought better of it as a logistical nightmare in terms of distribution, especially since dropping them from planes appeared foolhardy.

Newspapers and pamphlets were to be published and distributed in Albania by dropping them from planes. It was non-stop psychological warfare, with almost 100 million pamphlets dropped over a few years. Assuming everyone was illiterate, the pamphlets were mostly cartoons. Knowing absolutely nothing about what was going on in Albania, the propaganda seemed to have no effect whatsoever. There was a degree of hilarity to the whole business. In one drop, where the planes encountered anti-aircraft fire around Shkoder in the north and the central Albanian town of Elbasan, the planes also dropped food parcels and almost 500,000 leaflets. As a special gift to the Albanian mothers, packets of sewing needles were included as a token of help in "their untiring struggle to clothe their families against all the efforts of the communists to keep them naked and hungry." Sewing needles aside, most Albanians who encountered the material were afraid to even discuss it, knowing that there was a good chance their interlocutors were more likely informants than sympathizers.

On the island of Malta, training of guerillas was to begin in July 1949 in two steps: ten Albanians would be directly trained by American instructors; then these trainees would train another 40 Albanians selected by a sub-committee of the National Committee. These forty agents, largely taken from refugee camps, would be the commandos dropped into Albania by airplane or on the coast south of Vlora. Sadly, the training lasted only three weeks and most hardly knew how to be a paratrooper. Why the two-stepped approach? The Americans and the British wanted to preserve plausible deniability so the operation would not be traced back to them. An open attack on a Soviet satellite state could easily invite a Third World War. The second-to-last phase was to be the infiltration of the 40 agents with airdrops, beach landings, and overland border crossings. They had to establish communication, supply lines, and liaisons with existing resistance groups in Albania. Trouble was that there were no existing resistance groups left in Albania by then. The final phase, which eluded them, was an uprising against the government in an open insurgency. This was to happen *only* if the requirements were met and the conditions remained favorable. Infighting within the various groups meant that they could only agree on spheres of influence once they were successful. There would not be one Albania, but three.

In August 1949, the US-sponsored National Committee began a tour of Western capitals to rally support. Their first stop was Paris for the official announcement of the National Committee for a Free Albania, which was a front for the covert invasion of Albania. They went later to London, where they made a broadcast on the BBC. Then they began their American tour, which consisted of Washington, DC and New York City. But the New York City trip proved fatal for the committee. On October 3, 1949, one of the group's key leaders, Midhat Frashëri, was found dead in his hotel room on Lexington Avenue. The official cause of death was a heart attack, possibly brought on by the stress of the whole business. However, Frashëri's death was still considered somewhat suspicious. Described as healthy and

energetic, he showed no signs of poor health. Who did it? The Albanian secret police, known as the Sigurimi, did not have that type of reach. The Soviets did, though, and they were known to have the means to provoke heart
attacks in their victims. Frashëri's true cause of death remains unknown.
Zog never liked him.

Nevertheless, the plans for a rebellion continued. The US and UK
started running sorties inside the country for reconnaissance purposes
and to establish contacts with resistance leaders there. In October 1949, the
first official mission began. On a British Navy trawler, the Pixies were taken
from Malta to the coast of Italy to meet up with a Greek fishing boat called
the *Stormie Seas*. This vessel, complete with a husband and wife, a dog, and
a friend to look like a holiday trip, took the Pixies to the Albanian coastline. They landed on the isolated Karaburun Peninsula, just south of Vlora,
in very bad weather. They were to meet peasants who had been won over by
cartoons, recruit fighters, and start fomenting a revolution. However, their
reception was hardly what they expected. While villagers were often sympathetic, they were suspicious that so few people had come to overthrow the
government. Surely they would need more men, the locals concluded. A second landing took place on Albanian shores on October 10. However, four
of the twenty men put ashore during these first two missions were caught
and executed owing to operational shortcomings and Albanian foreknowl-
edge of the incursions. The rest were unsuccessful in recruiting other Albanians for their services. Most of the men spent their time on the run from
locals eager to report them to the communist secret police.

Word spread from village to village that several Albanian citizens had
been arrested or killed for helping them. But the Americans and the British
did not see this as a failure; a 20 percent casualty rate was not surprising, and
the agents had proved they could move around Albania and get in contact
with people. The agents spent their time almost entirely on the run, moving from village to village only to face constant rejection from the locals.
Clearly, the *besa* did not apply to Albanians coming to overthrow the government. It later emerged that the Sigurimi knew their every move, were
always on their tail, and knew where they would be. What nobody knew
was that Kim Philby had relayed the details of the plan from London to

the Soviets just as he was leaving the UK to take up his post as British liaison in Washington. Philby never denied his role in passing the secrets on to the USSR and would later recount from the safety of retirement in Moscow that he had no regrets for his role in thwarting a massacre in the Balkans. So successful was the Albanian counter-operation that they managed to seize even the radio equipment so that Albanian agents could easily pretend to be the foreign agents to further deceive and embroil the US and the UK in the operation.

By 1950, Hoxha's grip in Albania was surprisingly firm after such a relatively short time in power. This was a testimony to the success in creating a climate of permanent fear and distrust. It was more difficult for small guerrilla groups to move around in a nation that had slipped so easily into a terror regime. The memory of Xoxe was in the air too. In October 1950, sixteen men were sent in again. They had been trained in Germany but were given very little of it. The SIS was very eager to get them into Albania as soon as possible. But once again, the police were waiting for them. One of the men sent in, Adem Kjura, was wanted by the Sigurimi, but he escaped into Yugoslavia. After he escaped, the Albanian police tortured or murdered his whole family—forty people in total—in revenge. Kjura held Philby personally responsible for all those deaths. Another group that had landed at the same time crossed into Yugoslavia, recruited 15 people in Prizren, and came back to Albania. However, the Albanian police managed to pick them off one by one in various encounters by the spring of 1951. They were either killed or surrendered. If you surrendered, you got torture, then a show trial, and finally execution.

By 1951, the Pixies, unsurprisingly, felt like they were going into suicide operations, and doubts arose as to whether they'd ever be able to overthrow Hoxha as mission after mission proved to be failures. Still, despite constant failure, the US and UK persisted, unaware that there was a mole in the operation. Yet another round of 43 men was sent through again in 1951. The drop was a total disaster, and the police were waiting for them at their exact drop location. They were dropped in on July 23 and had all been quickly killed or captured. They included the remnants of Zog's royal guard, Kasem Shehu and Muhamet Hoxha, who went on trial in October 1951 in

Tirana. Hoxha and Shehu got twenty years; Iliaz Toptani and Selim Daci were given life in prison; and two others were sentenced to death. But they all probably died at some point in prison. The Sigurimi had known everything for the last two years.

In July 1951, Zog went to the US to start working closer with the CIA. He was growing tired of the British, and the US seemed to take him far more seriously. He stayed at the Ritz in Manhattan. He claimed he had come to the US to see modern civilization, but he was really there to help the CIA coordinate the overthrow of the Albanian communists. The CIA agreed to use some of Zog's own guards to continue trying to infiltrate Albania and establish contact with some Zogists there. The CIA still wanted to bring Zog to the United States so he could continue connecting them with agents to infiltrate Albania. However, prior to his departure, the Egyptian police raided his villa in Alexandria, seized papers, and told him he could not leave with his gold and jewels. The CIA also helped allay Zog's fears of jeopardizing his claim to the throne if he was perceived as giving up his citizenship by granting him entry into the US as an immigrant and waiving normal entry requirements in the "national interest."

In the fall of 1951, Zog bought the Knollwood estate in Muttontown, Long Island—a 256 acre property with a 60 room mansion. The local press said he paid for the property with a bucket of diamonds and rubies, but more reliable sources put the price at 102,000 USD. He hired a press agent, too, to help him open doors in the US State Department. He planned to move the whole family there, set up a feudal farm, and train commandos for more raids into Albania, although local media, with encouragement from a CIA-sponsored media campaign, said he planned to spend his remaining years as a country squire running a tiny replica of Albania inside the grounds. The locals loved it. Ironically, the caretaker of the property was a former soldier in Wrangel's White Army. Zog later ran into trouble when he refused to pay $3,000 in local taxes because, as a king, he insisted, he was immune from tax. Zog paid up but never lived there. Rumors persisted that he hid jewels there, which drove the locals into a destructive digging frenzy as they tore the place apart looking for Zog's buried treasure. The mansion slid into dilapidation. It was demolished in 1959. The jewels were never found.

Back in Egypt, Zog was getting desperate due to ongoing harassment from the Egyptian authorities. In August 1952, Zog tried to open another door to toppling Hoxha. It was 1924 all over again when he attempted to renew his cooperation with Yugoslavia by sending his emissaries to meet Tito's emissaries in Skopje, the Macedonian republic. The talks were by all accounts jovial, with great food and wine. Zog's people lied fantastically about the need to cooperate with Yugoslavia to make a better future for Albania. They all agreed to work together and to plan the next meeting at a much higher level with Zog personally, but that never occurred. In early 1953, one overoptimistic official in the US State Department's Southeast Europe Division suggested that planning commence for the post-Hoxha era.

Stalin's death in March 1953 emboldened hopes for Albania as the first domino to fall, but it again proved hopeless. The Americans got cold feet, the British could not afford to do it on their own, and the Greek communists had been defeated anyway, which radically diminished Albania's strategic importance. The Pixies felt betrayed—not just by Philby—but by their trusted mentors and sponsors, especially in the US. By late 1953, the Albanian communists had been handed a massive propaganda victory. They had all the evidence they needed to prove that the country was indeed encircled and that its enemies would stop at nothing to destroy it. That is what they had been saying all along. Zog, Albanian communist radio said, had not changed one bit; he was still in the service of foreign powers. He was nothing more than a satrap. There was that word again. Zog vowed again to commit suicide. Leka vowed revenge. That was the end of the incursion operations, although the leaflet and food aid drops continued.

1953 got grim for Zog's court in Egypt as Zog was effectively out of options, and it was decided to move to France. Worse still, Zog again found himself at the end of another dynasty—this time the Alis of Egypt. The free-spending, fast-driving, vulgar, and corrupt King Farouk was out in the Egyptian Revolution of 1952, when Egypt became a republic. Ever present at the wrong moments, Zog was again on the wrong side of history. Although they lacked the longevity of the Habsburgs, the Ali dynasty had certainly lasted longer than Zog's. Farouk was sent into exile in Italy in July 1952, and the gaggle of Balkan monarchs living in Egypt faced a very uncertain future, Zog especially, as Farouk was part Albanian, and this worked for Zog until it did not. Like the sultans of the old Ottoman Empire, Farouk was guarded by Albanians.

The new government had no interest in the likes of Zog milling around much longer and did their best to make life impossible for him and his entourage. Just like on Long Island, it came down to a question of taxes—Zog wasn't paying any as a king. For Egypt's new rulers, Zog was merely an anachronism. The new rulers would either shake him down for cash, customs duties, and back taxes or throw him out. The Egyptians started to make life difficult for him with a very well-coordinated harassment campaign. Luckily, given the ongoing operations in Albania, the US still deemed him an extremely valuable asset. The CIA and the US Embassy in Cairo did their best to save Zog by trying to convince Egypt's new rulers that vilifying Zog would hurt Egyptian prestige. The Egyptian government did not seem to care. The Egyptians also accused Zog of arms trafficking during the Israeli conflict. The CIA concluded that it was simply the Egyptian government trying to blackmail Zog and that the new government was under pressure from the Soviets to get rid of Zog as a favor to Hoxha. In August 1953, the Egyptians closed the Royal Albania Legation and declared their passports invalid. Overnight, in the Egyptian newspapers, King Zog became Mr. Zog. The Egyptian press later accused Zog of helping Farouk smuggle money out of Egypt. The US, through their ambassador in Cairo, did their best to help their "asset," telling the Egyptian authorities that Zog was an "important anti-communist symbol" and a key source of "infiltration agents" into Albania. The US kept the pressure up, but the Egyptians held firm.

In September 1953, the Egyptian authorities raided Zog's house, demanded access to his safe, and seized 9000 gold coins. In the end, Zog was told he could leave, but without the gold. The Egyptian Government maintained Zog never declared the cash in the first place and that he was involved in shady dealings largely around using his diplomatic status to import fine jewelry into Egypt tax-free and then selling it at enormous profits. Rumors also circulated that he owned a Ford car dealership. It turned out that he arrived in Port Said with 150,000 gold pieces, more than 180 kilograms, and was left with only 15,000 gold pieces in the end. The CIA sanctioned another press campaign in Egypt to paint Zog in a different light in the country. The CIA hoped that they could also put pressure on the Egyptians because of their respect for the organization and Zog's place as one of their assets.

Due to poor health and an inability to travel, Zog sat it out for another two years, suffering enormous fears of assassins arriving from Albania, before leaving Egypt for good to his final destination: France. More bad news came from the incursions into Albania. After a dramatic show trial in April 1954, more sentences were handed down. Shehi, Branica, Sul, and Malushi were sentenced to death by firing squad, while the ever elusive and slippery Majtani was publicly hanged. The judge said Matjani was fated "to suffer death by the cord." Sitting around the table listening to the death sentences on the radio was an important moment for the then fifteen-year-old Crown Prince Leka. Shehu and Branica had worked for his father. Vengeance was due. Blood could not be left unavenged. The joint American-British operations were a debacle. The Americans pulled the financial plug and dismissed the remaining agents waiting to be dropped into Albania.

After the 1954 trial of Shehu and Matjani, the communists took vengeance where it could hurt Zog the most: they killed about 400 people in Mati, Zog's ancestral homeland. The families of those condemned in the trial were shot, then the people whom Shehu and the others were supposed to contact were also killed. Shehu had given the secret police all the names under torture; then, when those were implicated, more were tortured. It is estimated that several thousand people died in total because of the operations—a lot for a population of only just over 1 million people. The message was read loud and clear. Who was to blame, then, for the operation's failure? Surely not Zog, who merely gave up his people to fight an unwinnable fight.

Finally, in May 1954, one month after they had been sitting around the kitchen table listening to his men's death sentences in Tirana, Zog was able to get his cash back owing to US pressure and he left for France with his entourage in 1955. In extremely poor health, Zog departed Egypt in total despair, knowing by then that his chances for a return to Albania were now zero. Some people told him to head for Nice, but he worried the place was cursed as the deposed Ottomans, even the last caliph, had once made their home there. The Americans had largely abandoned him, knowing that pushing Egypt to go easier on Zog was not worth it—they valued their relationship with Egypt far more, and there were bigger issues in the Middle East. Plus, for the sake of preserving an agent inside the government, Zog was cut loose for good. The gig was up and never again would he be approached for insight. In Tirana, the communists were emboldened; the jailing and executions continued. The borders, long closed, became even harder to get past and Albania opted for a hardline path that later set it apart from even the most repressive of the communist bloc states. How much did the folly of the poorly executed and costly interventions in Albania contribute to Albania's isolation? —Likely quite a bit. The Albanians settled into a long Stalinist night that did not end until the early 1990s.

While the UK and the US gave up on sending emigres into Albania, their psychological warfare continued and even intensified. More and more leaflets—some 25 million in 1954 and 1955 alone—and false flag operations continued. Special shortwave broadcasts intensified with detailed analysis and commentary on Hoxha's speeches. In the long run, the US hoped to convince the Albanians that the West still cared about them, and was still intent on causing trouble in the Tirana-Moscow axis and in keeping the Soviets occupied elsewhere. Harassment letters sent from Berlin to top communist officials started as well, containing incriminating messages written in invisible ink made detectable when held up to the light.

In the chaos that followed Stalin's death, a new order emerged in the communist world, one that had profound implications for Albania's rulers, who had always seen themselves as the only true believers. Ordinary Albanians, having lived through such routine violence, hoped the rumors were true that the terror would be eased. However, only the Albanians saw fit to deify Stalin forever. Slowly dying of cancer in the Villa Saint Blaise on the French Riviera, Zog found some hope in the changes that were coming out of the USSR. The new Soviet boss, Nikita Khrushchev, unleashed an almost casual re-evaluation of Stalin and Stalinism, focusing largely on some of the excesses in the not-so-secret speech of February 1956 that shook the entire communist world. The Albanians were furious with the debasement of Stalin. More worrying for the Albanians was that Khrushchev also softened the anti-Western rhetoric and spoke of peaceful coexistence. Khrush-

chev told Hoxha to slow down industrialization, rehabilitate a few comrades who had been sent to the gallows or who had been shot—including
Xoxe—make friends with Tito, and drift back into an emphasis on growing
things like olives and fruit. Hoxha wanted none of that. Digging up bodies of dead former comrades, especially Xoxe, was a dangerous business and
Hoxha knew it. It ate away at your legitimacy and could not be managed.
Stalin had saved them in 1948 and Stalinism, as far as they saw things, was
the only path to modernity and survival.

Zog watched, at first with elation, as the Hungarian attempt to fashion a humane socialism morphed into a revolution in October and November 1956. The Hungarians promised neutrality, democracy, and the end of
communism. This was just what he had hoped for when he bought into
the joint American-British plan to foment a revolution in Albania. In the
end, though, the status quo prevailed. The USSR could not allow Hungary
to chart a new course, and the Americans were unwilling to risk another
war for a place like Hungary. This time around, the US did not send people to foment the revolution; instead, leaflets were dispatched again urging the Hungarian resistance to fight. Based in Munich, Radio Free Europe
said help was on the way. The USSR sent troops, destroyed the revolution,
put in a puppet leader who stayed in power until 1988, and stood by later
as the revolution's leaders, all good communists, were summarily executed
and buried in unmarked graves waiting to be unearthed, literally and fig-
uratively, in 1989.

Outside of the clamor in the United Nations, the events in Hungary led
to nothing. The Americans had hoped to capitalize on Stalin's death as a catalyst for the collapse of communism but this failed completely. In Paris, Zog
was despondent. In Tirana, Hoxha, watchful and fearful, considered himself
warned. Hoxha must have been genuinely terrorized, given the fate of Hungary. Step out of line and get invaded then murdered. He too wanted a separate path, just not the same one as Hungary. Thus, something that seemed
impossible became real: the Albanians began a long divorce with Moscow
and a new marriage of convenience with the fellow hardline Stalinists in
Beijing. Thankfully, the USSR decided not to invade. For Hoxha, Albania
was thankfully deemed not worth the effort. Irrelevance was a new asset.

Chapter Eleven

Journeys Home

On April 9, 1961, Zog died at the Foch hospital in Paris. It was cancer. He was buried in Paris's Thiais Cemetery with a stark granite gravestone of three columns reading: "Fatherland Above All"—a favorite of his. He did not want to be buried in Albania until after the communists were gone, and, in any case, even if it had been his wish, the communists would have declined. Nobody, not even other exiled royalty, came to the funeral, so the Zog royal line seemed to be finished. Not long after, in another Bristol Hotel, but this time in Paris, the twenty-two-year-old Leka was crowned

Zog in exile, undated photograph

king, still promising revenge. The obituaries Zog would never see in *The Times* of London or the *New York Times* would be found on the back pages as afterthoughts for cocktail party chit chat. Mere curiosities in the "Where are they now?" file of dead Kings. Zog was just one of the many Balkan kings ousted during the Second World War and after, alongside the kings of Bulgaria, Romania, and Yugoslavia. They were left hoping that somehow the communists who took over would topple and they could return to a jubilant population.

How could he know that *The Times* would put him beside the death of a post-impressionist artist? That paper called him a dictator, "strong, efficient, and, where necessary, ruthless." They lauded his personal rule as just what the primitive Albanians needed. Expectations remained low, and Albania was even less known in 1961 than it had been when it appeared in 1912. The iron hand for lawless Albanians, just like always. *The New York Times* was less effusive, placing him next to the death of an obscure oil executive. When Atatürk, Turkey's great reformer and dictator, died in 1938, he was on page one. When Enver Hoxha died in 1985, he also got the front page of *The Times*. To its credit though, *The New York Times*, alone among the world's newspapers, appreciated how hard it had been to rule Albania in such horrible times between the First and Second World Wars. What the obituaries did not mention was that Zog was also devious, unscrupulous, and a murderer. The one and only paper of record in communist Albania, the *Voice of the People*, did not even mention Zog's death. He was not even yesterday's news. He had been written out of history, but since Zog never actually created any memories, it was easy. A unique possibility in the communist world, the cleansing of public memory in this instance could be skipped. He was a non-person in a place where the past was always evolving. He was extinct.

Not that Zog's death had anything to do with it, but even stranger things started to happen in Albania. Hoxha decided to go full-out with his China experiment, and throughout the 1960s Albania drifted closer and closer to China, eventually becoming a full-fledged satellite. Hoxha's reasons were simple: Stalinism was still the only game in town, and he rejected the Soviets for abandoning Stalin. The world, according to Hoxha, was split into two hostile blocs: the Soviets, who abandoned real Marxism-Leninism-

Stalinism and led the "revisionist" bloc, which had broken with the correct path, and the Americans, the perpetual enemy, who led the Imperialist bloc. Two adversaries, as Hoxha said, equally nasty and bent on Albania's destruction. The Albanians invested big in international broadcasting to tell the world of the real thing. Despite grinding poverty, money was sent to communist parties abroad that stuck to the Stalinist line.

In the rest of the communist bloc, in the aftermath of Stalin's death, the road to communism took varying paths. The Hungarians and the Poles tried to shake off the worst excesses but failed. The Hungarians had certainly gone the furthest in 1956, when they even attempted to exit the communist bloc and become a neutral state. The Soviet Army intervened and sent the reformists packing. The West did nothing. The new Hungarian government did not hesitate to execute them all later. In 1968, the Czechoslovaks tried a softer version of Hungary 1956, hoping for the impossible "socialism with a human face." The Soviets, this time with a few of their Warsaw Pact allies, came again, and Czechoslovakia went back to a form of neo-Stalinism that persisted well into the 1980s. After an enormous amount of bloodletting and emigration, the Hungarians ended up with "goulash communism," a form of social peace through consumerism and state-imposed amnesia. It was easier to stay out of jail if you just lied low, grabbed a bottle of state-made plum brandy, some cigarettes, and simply forgot that your prime minister had been executed or that what happened in 1956 was anything other than a foul counter-revolution.

In the Balkans, things were even more absurd. If the interwar leaders had been merely thieves, the communists were thieves *par excellence*. Yugoslavia's Tito built a luxurious empire with yachts, expensive cars, and palaces, allegedly having over 30 residences. Tito dressed in outrageous military uniforms. The cunning but totally uneducated Nicolae Ceausescu in Romania certainly took the cake for indulgence, vulgarity, and kitsch. Like Zog, Ceausescu had a food taster that he even brought on a visit to meet Queen Elizabeth II. Albania's leaders eschewed displays of wealth that went too far. Hoxha had three residences and a food taster as well. If a hierarchy of suffering under Balkan communism were to be made, the Albanians had it the worst by far, followed very closely by the Romanians.

In 1968, Hoxha turned sixty. Forty years before, an Albanian would have been perplexed by the appearance of Zog's initials, AZ, on a mountainside. The habit persisted as the country was later covered in slogans extolling work, discipline, and vigilance, glory to the Albanian communist party, or Long Live Comrade Enver. In 1968, to honor the country's "father," a gigantic ENVER appeared on Mount Shpirag, overlooking the southern town of Berat. The slope had been cleared of brush, then thousands of rocks were transported up the mountain in very challenging conditions. The rocks, painted white, made 150 meter tall and 60 meter wide letters. Albania's post-communist leaders later tried bombs and napalm to destroy it. A clever local artist later rearranged things to spell NEVER.

Despite spontaneous gratitude, the late 1950s and 1960s were precarious times. Hoxha knew that if he succumbed to change it would end badly for him; he had no wish to die if Albania had been forced to change course. China's break with the USSR over the same ideological skirmishes could not have come at a better time. The Soviet advisors were promptly sent home along with their navy and some of their precious submarines from Albania's strategic Adriatic coastline. The Chinese advisors came immediately. China had a colony of sorts in Europe. Chairman Mao gushed that even though the two countries were separated by "thousands of mountains and rivers, their hearts were linked, and together they would be victorious." Hoxha promised everlasting friendship. Taking a page from Zog's guide to survival, Hoxha never left Albania from 1961 onward.

Ordinary Albanians chafed at the new era and complained about the quality of Chinese products. There was no love lost between the two nations. Doubtless, it was tough for Albanians to be on the receiving end of Chinese aid. Taking orders from Russians was one thing, but not from the Chinese. In February 1967, Hoxha called on the youth especially to begin a fight against religion. Albania decided to have its own Cultural Revolution too, which, although decidedly less violent than the Chinese version, was marked by the strange decision to abolish Albania's three religions completely. It was, at least according to the party, a blow to a reactionary past that had only served to divide and enslave the Albanians and block their path to enlightened socialism and then communism. Communist youth went on rampages, destroying religious sites and desecrating graves. Churches and mosques were shuttered or made into cultural spaces, theatres, or youth clubs as Albania became the world's first atheist state. A delegation of Chinese Red Guards arrived to inspire Albania's heroic youth.

Later, the party opened up a Museum of Atheism which brought together an exceptionally strange collection of items. Unsurprisingly, the museum was in Shkoder, the center of Catholic life. Visitors were first greeted with Marx's slogan that "Religion is the opium of the people." The museum included a mannequin priest that was designed to prove to you that there was no truth to the lie that a saint's body did not decompose—all along you had been fooled. The focus though was on religion as a tool of foreign domination and a source of corruption and traitors. Oddly enough, even without the decree, Albanians were headed towards a kind of atheism anyway. Religion was never really their thing. As a special added treat, given that not everyone accepted such radical change, Hoxha waged another war on gossiping as a sign of being opposed to the party.

In those odd times, getting in or out of Albania became even harder. Like any communist bloc state, foreign travel was highly restricted to the party faithful who could be trusted to keep to themselves what they might have seen in the West. In the 1960s, a certain Albanian-born nun started to think about a return to Albania to see her mother and sister. Mother Teresa, like Zog, was born in the Ottoman Empire and left Albania in 1928. She had never been back. Given the nature of Hoxha's attitude toward religion, Mother Teresa's family hid their connection to the famous nun in Calcutta. Already in the 1960s, Mother Teresa sought permission for her sister to travel to Italy for urgent medical care. The Albanian Embassy in Rome never bothered to answer, so she tried the Vatican. Still nothing came from Tirana. She later tried to get a visa to Albania to see her mother and sister. Despite pleas from French president De Gaulle, Jackie Kennedy, and others, Hoxha would not permit a dangerous religious activist into Albania. Mother Teresa's mother died in 1972, her sister in 1973. Like Zog's mortal remains and Leka, Mother Teresa also needed to wait for the communists to fall from power before she could return in 1991.

The Chinese proved to be better benefactors than the Soviets. For certain, they had less money to throw around, but they were far enough away that they would never have even dreamed of invading Albania the way the Soviets invaded Hungary in 1956 or Czechoslovakia in 1968 because of ideological transgressions. Brand China did not do invasions. But the love affair with China eventually ended too. Whether planned or not, Hoxha decided that the purest form of Marxism-Leninism-Stalinism could only be preserved by simply going it alone. Total self-reliance and more grass eating when necessary. First there was the rapprochement with the United States and President Nixon's visit to China, which really rankled Hoxha. He told Mao as much, but in the gentlest of terms. The US and the USSR were simply common enemies—full stop. Then Chairman Mao died in 1976 and the Albanian communists were devastated when more moderate voices prevailed. But things went too far when Deng Xiaoping started on about enriching yourselves, and Hoxha told the Chinese advisors to get lost. Albanian students studying in China were ordered home immediately. "Everlasting friendship" ended abruptly. Hoxha routinely denounced the pompous Deng. They had betrayed the cause. By 1978, Albania was the paragon of isolation. As the price for the dogmatic adherence to Stalinism, Albanians just got poorer and poorer as the gap between them and the rest of the world just got bigger and bigger.

But nobody could even guess what absurdities still lay ahead in the precarious dog-eat-dog world of the Albanian Communist Party. No doubt those brave enough were hinting that maybe the go-it-alone policy needed to be rethought. Everything was in short supply, and the queues for food were just getting longer and longer. Inside the party, dissent was hardly welcome. The party line could not change, and Hoxha set about ensuring continuity for his eventual death.

December 17, 1981 was a very bad day for Mehmet Shehu, the Albanian prime minister and the number two in a near hierarchy of one since 1949, after Koçi Xoxe was put in front of a firing squad and removed from Albanian history. Shehu would soon be written out of Albanian history too. In the communist world, you died first by a bullet or the noose, then a second death came when you were removed from the past. If you were lucky, you could be resurrected when and if the party line changed to show that maybe you had been right after all. In any case, one last great purge was on the books, and the prime minister was set to move from perpetrator to victim in a matter of months. In the Albanian communist world since 1948, Shehu was the henchman, torturer-in-chief, and very bad cop to Hoxha's mere bad cop persona.

It came down to something petty, just like always: a bad biography. In August, Shehu's middle son said he wanted to get married, and the father gave his approval. His mistake was forgetting to ask Hoxha, who eventually concluded that the child was set to marry the wrong person—a daughter of class enemies banished to the margins of Albania. Hoxha at first welcomed the marriage, but then changed his mind and insisted the whole thing be called off. From September 1981, Shehu's career took dramatic turns for the worse. Hoxha toyed with him, loving him one day, hating him the next. Hoxha's wife needled him in turn, chastising him as weak for not getting rid of Shehu and his bloodsucking family. The 73-year-old Hoxha was already demented by then. In power for too long, the decisions he made were increasingly irrational. The break with China and the pursuit of self-reliance had only served to widen the gap between Albania and the rest of Europe. His underlings could hardly gauge how to react in his presence. Did you look him in the eye? That risked Hoxha perceiving conspiracy there or doubt. To not look, to avoid eye contact, invited the same conclusion. What a conundrum. In the last years of the dictator's life there was no way to gauge where you stood. The Politburo was a circus as the men around the table sought to undo one another in sycophancy. While ordinary Albanians sat under one light bulb watching state TV, preparing to get up early to join a queue for food, the "blockmen," as they were called, since they lived in a secluded block of Tirana that no ordinary Albanian could ever dream of seeing, enjoyed their special status poolside or playing billiards as their wives looked on. They felt secure in their futures. They had no foreign bank accounts, or even domestic ones. The future was theirs.

Shehu became the scapegoat for everything. By December, his time was up. The party needed a major sacrifice to start what was to be a final and dramatic purge of alleged enemies for the forthcoming post-Hoxha era. The final curtain was about to fall as the dictator tried to prove to his wife that he still had it in him to deliver more death. On December 17, Shehu showed up at work on what would be his last day as prime minister. He was called out for the usual stuff: betraying the revolution and abandoning the class struggle. Shehu repented and tried to make things right. Even more self-criticism was expected and he did what he was told, throwing himself on the mercy of Hoxha and the circle of toadies who smelled blood, upward mobility, and perks. Shehu had a posh villa in Tirana's secluded block (the inaccessible part of Tirana with what by any standard were magnificent homes equipped with everything), a beach house in Durres, and another near Vlora. Confronted, then humiliated and exposed, at least as the story goes, Shehu went home and shot himself in the head. What choice did he have? He was found with a pistol beside his bed. Nobody really knows what happened that night. Suicide was an extremely hard sell, but there was a note where Shehu professed his loyalty to his master and the great communist cause. Suicide actually made sense. Either he killed himself or he would be executed. Like Koçi Xoxe, his final reflections suggested he knew why he had to die. A near 40-year friendship and 27 years as prime minister meant nothing. Shehu begged Hoxha to look after his family. Hoxha did the opposite by arresting his family. An ordinary and anodyne obituary appeared on December 18, listing Shehu's service to the cause, but no mention of suicide. But by the end of the day, things got murkier when it was announced to the Albanian public that Shehu killed himself in a moment of "nervous crisis." What were people to think when a prime minister kills himself? Rumors persisted that he was shot during a Politburo meeting. What were Albanians to think? Almost everyone alive had grown up under the rule of these two men. Now what?

An engagement gone bad was later rolled out as a far bigger scandal as Hoxha clamored to use Shehu's suicide to clean house, largely at his wife's urging, who had to ensure that her life after Hoxha would go on as just as it had. Albanians were living under terror once again and Shehu was buried almost without mourners. Who would take the risk of showing up? The party invented a terrific lie to justify Shehu's end. He was behind a massive movement to overthrow Albanian socialism. For 40 years, the prime minister was working with foreign intelligence services. A state-sponsored panic ensued: Albania stood at a precipice with Shehu's accomplices still at large. Everyone was a potential enemy. The whole thing meant that Hoxha cleared the party of fake enemies and saw off a man he became convinced was set to destroy him and his family. One time Politburo members, at the very top echelon of the party, were reduced to disgraced criminals begging for forgiveness. Those spared the macabre madness got in line to heckle, laugh at, and scorn their one-time friends at what were absurdist show trials presided over by Hoxha. By then, Hoxha was demented and sick with diabetes, but nobody stood in his way.

In 1982, Shehu was publicly denounced for unspeakable crimes over the entirety of his service to Albanian communism. Word went out that Shehu had to be stricken from the public record until new books were produced. The elite took the books off their shelves, the official histories, and redacted Shehu everywhere or simply cut the pages out and burned them. Personal photos with him were destroyed or his face merely scratched out with a fingernail, lest cherished family photos ended up in the stove.

Leka saw an opportunity with the chaos in the top echelons. Barely a year later, Leka claimed responsibility for an impromptu invasion à la Pixies in the 1950s hoping to take advantage of the intra-party infighting, but later denied he was responsible. In any case, the Albanians claimed the invaders were liquidated immediately. Leka did not deny that he had his people working in Albania on sabotage operations. Nobody knows what happened, but Hoxha used the invasion for even more violence. In 1983, three top officials were executed. Others received lengthy prison sentences. For Hoxha, in his demented mind, he assumed top people were aiming to replace him and destroy his family. He needed to ensure his power but also find a successor that would leave his family's privileges intact and his place in Albanian history unmolested. The de-Stalinization that followed Stalin's death had to be avoided.

In April 1985, Hoxha died. First, the men of the Politburo started bawling, then an entire nation joined them in what were sometimes real displays of grief. Seven days of mourning followed as school kids furiously wrote a poem or two about the legacy of Uncle Enver. Ramiz Alia, a total mediocrity who emerged as the main beneficiary of Shehu's tortured end, was party boss and he had to do whatever Enver's widow told him to do. The plus side of the murder or jailing of other top communists was that it opened up all kinds of possibilities for middle-brow losers like Alia.

Monumental but unforeseen changes in the Soviet Union in the mid-1980s opened a series of possibilities, and Poland led the way out of the darkness. Isolated, it appeared Albania might make the last stand and somehow preserve its unique brand of communism. Self-reliance gave way to massive poverty and despair. More akin to North Korea than anywhere else in the communist world, it seemed like Albania's communism just might survive.

Leka had an idea in early 1990 to break the last Stalinist holdout with a plan for a balloon invasion. Hardly original given what the CIA and MI6 had done in the 1950s, Leka decided to send thousands of helium-filled balloons with pamphlets urging his people to start a revolution. Leka also floated leaflets in bags down the rivers from Yugoslavia. The leaflets included a color photo of Leka in military dress with a machine gun standing in front of his "army." He did have one new advantage, though, as by this time the Albanians were almost all literate and could read the calls to resist. However, by early 1990, it hardly mattered—even the communists there threw in the towel and allowed somewhat free elections to take place in March 1991. Albania again bucked the trend in Europe when it became the only post-communist country to elect communists in its first free elections.

The peasants could hardly be blamed for fearing a return to private property and the feudalism of the Zog days that they had learned about in schools and heard about from parents and grandparents alike. Chaos, strikes, and a mass exodus followed the elections, and the Albanians went to the polls again in 1992. This time the communists, who in a strangely accepted sleight of hand became socialists, lost and Albania, largely from scratch, tried to build a democracy. The question of a return to a kingdom was an open one, but hardly anyone could even imagine Albania as a kingdom again. The other kings of the Balkans wanted back too, but they all seemed so drearily pathetic and anachronistic. Could they not just go away? A life in exile was hardly an alibi for no experience, and most of the sons and daughters of the kings and queens chose to forget that their parents

had botched things badly with a legacy of quashed constitutions, kleptocracy, and dictatorship. Everyone, except their jaded offspring, knew that.
In Albania, where another unassailable truth replaced the old unassailable
truth, a few people must have wondered that maybe the time of the king
had not been so bad after all.

Not long after being crowned king in 1961, Leka left France for Spain
under the relative protection of Spanish dictator Francisco Franco and
a friendship with King Juan Carlos I. He also developed close ties with the
Shah of Iran and the Saudi royal family. Franco died in 1975 and Leka's days
were numbered. He was eventually kicked out of Spain in 1979 for arms
trafficking. Leka claimed that external pressure forced Spain to expel him
and his small army. Alongside an enormous cache of weapons, Leka settled
briefly in Rhodesia before it became Zimbabwe and its new leader, Robert
Mugabe, made it abundantly clear that he preferred Tirana's communist
leaders to the rightist gunrunner holed up on a farm near Harare. His near
final stop was apartheid-era South Africa, where his love of guns continued
and he plotted revolution back home. Since nothing big came out of the
chaos that resulted from Mehmet Shehu's suicide, Leka kept trying to get
back his throne. He claimed, without proof, that he was using his bases in
Spain and later South Africa to train soldiers for an overthrow.

Many people were desperate enough to believe that maybe a king could
bring money, and lots of it, in an era when a population so deprived of information could easily imagine that a century of misery could be ended by
a single rich person. Rumors of the king's extraordinary wealth captivated
thousands. Albania was inundated with scams, get-rich-quick schemes, grift-
ers, and every form of religious infiltration you could think of. The long
cut-off diaspora—some good, some bad—returned home. It was open season
on 3 million people looking for a new God. They went from no choice to
too much choice in a matter of weeks. In a country run entirely by rumors
after years of total isolation, voices spoke of Albania's gold finally coming
home—and it would be enough for everyone. Albania could become the
next Switzerland in a matter of years. They heard Leka was super rich and
connected with all the real monarchs, especially the Saudi dynasty, and for
certain they had the cash to remake Albania. Besides, Albania needed a pa-

tron; it had always had one—Italians, Serbs, Russians, and Chinese. Whatever Albania's achievements, they had always been paid for by someone else. The period without a benefactor proved to be a fiasco. Mostly secular Albanians bristled at links with the Islamic world—the abolition of religion in 1967 and years of state-sponsored atheism added up to something, and they hardly relished the thought of veils and mosques. They did see an opportunity to get cash from the Saudis and hoped they could get it without the proselytizing and a bonanza of new mosque construction. They would be proven wrong when Albania got only shabby-looking mosques and no cash.

Rumors were out of control. There was even more talk that negotiations were underway to move Israel to Albania, as Zog had envisioned in the 1930s. The Jews were coming again to save Albania. More rumors circulated that the six-foot, eight-inch King Leka was sighted. Some said he was starting to move among the people in disguise, testing the waters for his return. Tirana's tiny airport, with its palm-tree lined walkway to the tarmac designed only to receive communist dignitaries, was buzzing with news of the imminent return too. The king would sneak in and work from the inside to foment a groundswell of support for his return. Tall people were pulled aside, and a border guard would whisper, "Are you the king?" Sure enough, in 1993, Leka returned to Albania on a plane loaned to him by King Hussein of Jordan. Using a phony passport issued by his "royal court" in exile that said his occupation was "King of the Albanians," he never left the airport's tiny VIP lounge. The Albanian authorities were happy to admit him, just not on that passport. He was an Albanian after all—just not their king—but they never denied he was a citizen. Refusing an Albanian passport, he was kicked out of his country for the second time. He returned to South Africa to wait for something bad to happen in Albania. He needed the Albanians—and Albania—to get desperate. He needed them to sink so low into a morass that they would have to turn to him.

He did not have long to wait. Albania's transition to democracy in the 1990s proved to be more challenging than many had hoped; it was hardly easy to shake off five decades of madness and wild paranoia. Whatever the other obvious shortcomings of Albanian Stalinism, the propaganda machine had largely convinced most people that Albania had achieved something special. Since so few people had ever left the place, they could hardly be blamed for thinking like that. When confronted with reality, anger was hardly surprising. Freedom, as it turned out, was fraught with extraordinary challenges, and Albania stood a very real chance of becoming a failed state. Albania's new "democratic" leaders had hardly any democratic credentials, and things largely went badly as vengeance trumped good policy. For many, exit was the best option as thousands of people piled onto rusting boats in Durres that had been commandeered to sail for a new life in Italy. Inside Albania, many of the trappings of the old system remained, and the politics of vengeance prevailed. The blood feud, dormant to a degree, was back. The employees of the communist state, including much of the army, all got fired and new loyalists were found who had absolutely no qualifications outside of blind loyalty to the new party in power. Capitalism, as preached by the well-paid and well-heeled international advisors, was nasty as the former communists easily converted political power into economic power.

Albanians looked for easy ways out. Plus, a nasty form of gangsterism arrived, with loads of unemployed youth roaming the streets in balaclavas and shaking everyone down. Having lost so much time, Albanians were in a rush to get fat and rich or simply get out of the country. The new post-communist government was a darling of the West for its adherence to the internationally sanctioned plan to exit communism. They looked away when their opponents were murdered or jailed. Low expectations, shaped in 1914 when Wilhelm of Wied first arrived, had hardly changed.

As Albania slipped easily into another kind of dictatorship, Leka could only watch with glee from South Africa. A descent into chaos was just what he hoped for as he awaited his moment. While his father had waited for the collapse of communism, Leka waited for the collapse of Albania's experiment with democracy. He had a political party in Albania that promoted the return of the monarchy as a source of unity, but the average age of party members hovered around 70. It was mostly a party of diaspora: old, tired men in bad suits who had no lived experience of Albanian communism, just some tedious history lessons of a golden era under Albania's one true king. Albania's embrace of capitalism was unprecedented in post-communist Europe, and indeed Albanians traveled further and faster in their post-communist experience than any other country. It was like a brush fire as sleepy and serene Tirana, nestled beneath the beauty of Mount Dajti and free of cars because private car ownership had been banned, turned into a veritable carnival of big and small entrepreneurs, big- and small-time crooks, choking on the fumes of thousands of second-hand Mercedes plying the city's few bad roads. A ground-floor apartment with a balcony was a godsend—easily converted into a kiosk with smokes, candies, and warm soda.

The communists had made a few additions to the Tirana that Zog built with Italian money. With cash from the USSR, they had built a national library, a theater, an opera, and a national museum that was famous for its majestic mosaic above the main entrance portraying the Albanians— from the Illyrians to gun-toting communist partisans—hacking their way through history, just as Hoxha said they had and would, against all obstacles towards a bright socialist future that came to nothing. A 12-meter-tall statue of Enver Hoxha dominated the square for barely two years until anticommunist demonstrators brought it down in February 1991 in what was Albania's breaching of the Berlin Wall moment.

By 1994, with three years of wild capitalism, a once serene Tirana was almost destroyed by the rampages of a distraught population chasing every possible get rich scheme. The charm of a once tidy, nearly car-free capital with its citizens out for a nightly stroll on the main boulevard had been lost to illegal buildings, kiosks, cafés, restaurants, and used Mercedes jamming the streets. Public space completely disappeared. The tiny Lana River that ran through the city became a toilet. Everyone was selling something. Pensioners had the rug pulled completely out from under them and found themselves forced to sell small clutches of flowers, a handful of sunflower seeds, or stand in the heat by the family scale charging one leke, the Albanian currency, to weigh yourself. Peasants fled the poor villages in the north to find a new life in new shanty towns that appeared like mushrooms on the outskirts of Tirana. Fast money was the order of the day and, unsurprisingly, pyramid schemes arrived that preyed on greed and the fear of missing out after missing out for your whole life. Two generations were lost already.

While the collapse of communism changed some things, the arrival of bananas changed everything when they started arriving in boatloads from

Columbia. The first big pyramid scheme was indeed a quirky one that revolved around bananas and more. Bananas were simply unheard of in communist Albania, so their arrival in 1992 created a frenzy. Until then, the communists, in their quest for total self-reliance, claimed, as the slogan went, that Albanians were prepared to eat grass if it kept them from dependency again. That meant no bananas.

In 1991, Albanians found themselves without food, and the Italians and others had to step in with emergency food aid. Some savvy distributor sold bananas to hundreds and hundreds of micro-distributors who then hit the streets with as few as three or four bananas and nothing else except maybe some sunflower seeds rotting on an upturned box on a street corner. But the whole business merely enriched the top people and allowed Albania's new business elite, largely former communists with the right connections, to launch Albania's newfound role in the drug trade. The harmless banana that had avoided Albania told part of a bigger story as it allowed Albania to become a key gateway for drugs from Columbia and elsewhere in Latin America when it was shipped in containers. In the Albania of the 1990s, ports were controlled by political parties as part of a revenue stream staffed by desperate people in a country where a small amount of money could get someone murdered.

Esad Pasha's pre-First World War dream of a wonderful grey zone, where everyone was for sale and the borders fluid, was finally fulfilled. If the communist government had controlled every decision, especially as it related to foreign trade, the post-communist leaders proved completely incapable of developing other institutions to deal with the demands of a market economy. Judges, police, and other officials were easy to buy off. As a result, corruption took root, as did organized criminal groups that found Albania an easy place to thrive. In the 1990s, Albania emerged as a haven for all kinds of trafficking. In the so-called transition, powerful local mafias also emerged. Plus, the mass exodus of mostly young men who fled Albania in 1991 and after provided the basis for a willing and desperate labor force, largely in Italy, to take over critical distribution roles.

With a series of wars that started in Yugoslavia in 1992 and international sanctions added later, Albania made a seamless leap from North Korea on the Adriatic to a key component in the international smuggling trade. While the banana impoverished the small seller when the product went bad, those at the top found themselves awash in drug cash that needed to be laundered. International sanctions served to create several possibilities for adventurous and entrepreneurial Albanians to evade sanctions. For some ordinary people, smuggling became essential for survival. The drug groups took over illegal fuel and weapons exports to neighboring Yugoslavia. In the country's north, opening a gas station was a ticket to financial freedom. Weapons also moved seamlessly through Albania's ports. While the banana eventually left its place on the street and went to the store shelves, the import of bananas still played a key role in the arrival of drugs from Columbia. Albania essentially became and remained Europe's only narco-state.

That made cash a problem. There was so much of it in Albania that it had to go somewhere. Between 1995 and 1997, things got progressively weirder in Albania. Outwardly, it seemed a success story, and most outside observers were shocked by the alacrity with which Albanians adapted to an entirely different world. They were, according to the international advisors holed up in new five-star hotels on Tirana's main boulevard, simply the best capitalists. Beneath the façade of a sham democracy, however, were some very bad economic fundamentals that caught the attention of a few international advisors but which the government chose to ignore, since they were too dependent on the very bad fundamentals for cash to say anything. Simply put, they needed the cash to buy votes in the 1996 election. What happened between 1995 and 1997 was one of the cautionary tales of the post-communist transition. Several investment companies appeared that started to offer extraordinary interest rates to people. Things started slowly as people started to pile money into the schemes. As the money flowed in, the interest rates just went up and up.

The schemes were simply too good to be true and almost 70 percent of Albanians invested in them. Wives berated their husbands to make an investment as they watched their neighbors prosper. People liquidated every asset—house, car, horse, cow, or donkey—to put cash in when interest rates were more than 10 percent per month and they just went up and up as new schemes entered the market. Tirana was a new Las Vegas on the Adriatic as the cash just flowed and flowed until it stopped. Tirana's first democratic government in the entire twentieth century used the cash from the schemes to buy reelection in 1996. They won by the usual landslide, with 122 out of 140 seats.

In 1997, the whole edifice collapsed as it had to, and the fragile postcommunist Albanian society collapsed with it. Rival gangs took control and Albania fell into what some called a civil war. The army disintegrated, weapons depots were looted, which often went directly to organized criminal groups, and for a few months in 1997 Albania simply had no government whatsoever as gangs fought for control over territory. You could buy a gun for 20 dollars or even a tank. Even Tirana's airport authorities had to fight to save it from being seized by rebels. The Albanians had proven themselves ungovernable once again. Some 2000 people were killed in the fighting. Foreign nationals were evacuated. More than 1 billion dollars simply disappeared and was never found again. Nobody got their money back.

The chaos brought an opportunity for the exiled king. In April 1997, an Arab Wings charter plane arrived at Tirana's airport during the worst moments of chaos. As Albania's borders disappeared simply because there was no one around to secure them, the king finally came home when there was nobody left to check a passport. He was determined to restore the monarchy, even if it meant by force. Some 2,000 supporters, mostly old men or bored and exclusively male youth, showed up chanting "Long live the King." A few more lined the streets giving the Mussolini/Zog fascist salute. Leka in some ways looked totally out of his depth with his imperfect Albanian and lack of local knowledge, but he fit the moment in other ways after he traded his suits for a beret and camouflage gear with guns and grenades hanging from him. He also inherited his father's anti-charisma. Leka surrounded himself with a dubious and sinister-looking armed entourage in leather vests and cheap sunglasses, firing wildly in what Leka later justified as the way Albanians show happiness. He met the nation's embattled leadership, toured the country, and headed north to Burgajet in a dated government-loaned Mercedes limousine led by the usual retinue of gun-toting thugs. He hoped to revive the tribal loyalty of his late father's stomping ground. With so many guns around, Leka had no trouble finding idle males to take the equivalent of 5 USD to help him launch a civil war or line the streets chanting, "Long live the King!" The total absence of women at any rally was telling. Given that most people that had lived under his father's soft tyranny were dead, Leka decided he could safely promise to reunify the Albanians living in Kosovo, then under the very hard tyranny of Serbian leader Slobodan Milošević. Leka chose to ignore that his father had been one of the key figures in destroying the movement for Kosovo's liberation with a series of murders in the 1920s and 1930s. But Leka swept everything under the carpet. He would bring the Albanians of Greece, Kosovo, North Macedonia, and Montenegro together.

His rampage in northern Albania was short. There was no way Leka could have headed south, where the Albanians there hated both him and the monarchy. He would have been hanged. He was promised a referendum on the restoration of the monarchy which happened in June 1997. After losing badly even in such perfect circumstances, Leka denounced the referendum as rigged and, like his father, decided to shoot his way to the top. But he had not learned his father's knack for surgical assassination. Instead, he launched a very poorly organized attempt at a coup with the usual rent-a-crowd of male supporters. After an illegal rally in Tirana's main square, they menacingly set off for the offices of the Central Election Commission. At a time when Albania desperately needed peace, the king brought more violence because violence was the only thing he knew. When the Albanian prosecutor later charged him with being an organizer and participant in an armed uprising to overthrow the constitutional order in Albania and for inciting violence, he fled the country again to cool off back in South Africa. The Albanians talked about extradition but later accepted that it was better to leave Leka in Johannesburg. He blew his one chance. Just like his father, he was later sentenced in absentia, although Zog was sentenced twice in absentia—once by Fan Noli in 1924 and again by the communists. Leka was a national embarrassment—there was no denying that. Two Zogs, three forced exiles, and two jail sentences. The case for the monarchy was closed. In a fit of kindness, the charges were later dropped, and in 2002 he was allowed to return to live out his life in Albania as long as he stayed out of politics, which he largely did. On his third and final return, only 500

Zog's statue in Tirana
Photo by Artan R. Hoxha, 2023

supporters were there to greet him at the airport. He died an ordinary citizen in Tirana in November 2011. The international media, calling him the pretender to the throne, spoke of his arms collections and the stupidity of 1997. The Zog dynasty, for what it was, finished for good.

One year later, in November 2012, more than two decades after the communists left power, Zog's remains left the cemetery in France and returned home on the 100th anniversary of Albanian independence. It was technically not 100 years, given the occupation in the two world wars. Zog finally got a modest statue at three meters tall and a boulevard named after him—the very same one he had named after himself in the 1930s—Boulevard Zog I. After nearly fifty years of communist historical manipulation and in the subsequent quest to find something worth celebrating in the catastrophic twentieth century, many of Zog's transgressions were forgiven or at least swept under the carpet. He was a citizen again. He got a royal tomb too, a replica of the one he built for his mother in 1935. It was not a massive crypt filled with curious school kids eager to rub the sword of Albania's first, or maybe second, or even third king, but, given his somewhat humble beginnings among the apples in Burgajet, it had been quite a life. Nobody could deny that.

Suggested Readings

Abrahams, Fred C. *Modern Albania: From Dictatorship to Democracy in Europe.* New York: NYU Press, 2015.

Austin, Robert C. *Founding a Balkan State: Albania's Experiment with Democracy, 1920–1925.* Toronto: University of Toronto Press, 2012.

Austin, Robert C. *Making and Remaking the Balkans: Nations and States Since 1878.* Toronto: University of Toronto Press, 2019.

Carver, Robert. *The Accursed Mountains: Journeys in Albania.* London: Flamingo, 1999.

Fevziu, Blendi. *Enver Hoxha: The Iron Fist of Albania.* London, New York: I.B. Tauris, 2016.

Fischer, Bernd J. *Albania at War, 1939–1945.* West Lafayette: Purdue University Press, 1999.

Fischer, Bernd J., and Oliver Jens Schmitt. *A Concise History of Albania.* Cambridge: Cambridge University Press, 2022.

Fischer, Bernd J., ed.. *Balkan Strongmen: Dictators and Authoritarian Rulers of Southeast Europe.* London: Hurst, 2006.

Fischer, Bernd J. *King Zog and the Struggle for Stability in Albania.* Boulder: East European Monographs, 1984.

Glenny, Misha. *The Balkans: Nationalism, War, and the Great Powers, 1804–1999.* New York: Penguin, 2001.

Guy, Nicola. *The Birth of Albania: Ethnic Nationalism, the Great Powers of World War I and the Emergence of Albanian Independence.* London: I.B. Tauris, 2012.

Heaton-Armstrong, Duncan. *The Six Months Kingdom: Albania 1914.* London: Bloomsbury, 2005.

Hoxha, Artan R. *Communism, Atheism and the Orthodox Church of Albania: Co-operation, Survival and Suppression, 1945–1967.* London: Routledge, 2022.

Hoxha, Artan R. *Sugarland: The Transformation of the Countryside in Communist Albania.* Budapest: Central European University Press, 2023.

Lampe, John R., and Ulf Brunnbauer, eds. *The Routledge Handbook of Balkan and Southeast European History.* London: Routledge, 2020.

Logoreci, Anton. *The Albanians: Europe's Forgotten Survivors.* Boulder: Little-hampton Book Services, 1977.

Malcolm, Noel. *Rebels, Believers, Survivors: Studies in the History of the Albanians.* Oxford: Oxford University Press, 2020.

Mazower, Mark. *The Balkans: A Short History.* New York: Weidenfeld and Nicholson History, 2002.

Mëhilli, Elidor. *From Mao to Stalin: Albania and the Socialist World.* Ithaca: Cornell University Press, 2017.

Pavlowitch, Stevan K. *A History of the Balkans 1804–1945.* London: Routledge, 2014.

Pearson, Owen. *Albania and King Zog, 1908–1939.* London: I.B. Tauris, 2004.

Robyns, Gwen. *Geraldine of the Albanians: The Authorized Biography.* London: Frederick Muller Ltd, 1987.

Roselli, Alessandro. *Italy and Albania: Financial Relations in the Fascist Period.* London, New York: Bloomsbury, 2006.

Salleo, Ferdinando. *A Prince Too Far: The Great Powers and the Shaping of Modern Albania.* Washington, D.C.: New Academia Publishing LLC, 2016.

Schwandner-Sievers, Stephanie, and Bernd J. Fischer, eds. *Albanian Identities: Myth and History.* Bloomington: Indiana University Press, 2002.

Skendi, Stavro. *The Albanian National Awakening.* Princeton: Princeton University Press, 1967.

Swire, J. *Albania: The Rise of a Kingdom.* London: Williams and Norgate, 1929.

Tomes, Jason. *King Zog of Albania: Europe's Self-Made Muslim Monarch.* New York: NYU Press, 2003.

Vickers, Miranda. *The Albanians: A Modern History.* London: I.B. Tauris, 2014.

Name Index